cameras west

by Frank Manchel

Illustrated with photographs

PRENTICE-HALL, INC., Englewood Cliffs, N. J.

Cameras West by Frank Manchel
Copyright © 1971 by Frank Manchel

J92 ISBN-0-13-112730-6
Library of Congress Catalog Card Number: 73-146960
Printed in the United States of America J

Prentice-Hall International, Inc., London
Prentice-Hall of Australia, Pty. Ltd., Sydney
Prentice-Hall of Canada, Ltd., Toronto
Prentice-Hall of India Private Ltd., New Delhi
Prentice-Hall of Japan, Inc., Tokyo

Other Books by Frank Manchel

Movies and How They Are Made
When Pictures Began to Move
When Movies Began to Speak
Terrors of the Screen

To my mother Olga, in loving memory

"The bravest battle that ever was
fought,
Shall I tell you where and
when?
On the maps of the world
you'll find it not,
It was fought by the
mothers of men."

JOAQUIN MILLER

contents

SAINTS AND SINNERS

For more than seventy years, people everywhere have thrilled to cinematic adventures depicting the conquest of the American West. Hardly a person now living has not seen some film about frontiersmen like Daniel Boone, Jim Bowie, Davy Crockett, Kit Carson, "Buffalo Bill" Cody, "Wild Bill" Hickok, and Bat Masterson. These romanticized heroes represent for millions of viewers the ideals of courage, manhood and justice. Yet no critic can pinpoint why Westerns have such a continuing mass appeal.

One reason may be that audiences are fascinated with the wildness of men and with the wilderness of the American frontier. Wide-open spaces and untamed lands have existed since the beginning of man, and certainly there have always been brave and dauntless individuals who have risked their lives for fame and fortune. But rarely in recorded history has such a brief period of time—from roughly 1839 to 1889—produced so much destructive power: anarchy, violence, brutality and killing.

1

Another reason may be the dramatic struggle between the individual and the land. The American pioneer saw in his westward trek a chance to measure his strength against the forces of man and nature. His every effort was fraught with danger and hardship—from the unrelenting climate to the proud Indian defending his rights. Across thousands of miles, a pioneer knew that each step he advanced toward the frontier brought him closer to a new crisis and the grave. But he also believed that if he could endure the ordeal, there was an easy fortune waiting for him. Never before had men worked so dangerously for such easy riches. And we who watch from the security of our seats delight in deluding ourselves that we would have survived where weaker men had failed.

Still another reason for the western film's perennial success may be in the morality of the characters themselves. Committed as we are to a civilized society founded on rules and regulations, to a government which sometimes moves exceedingly slow in punishing the guilty and defending the innocent, each of us finds a sense of satisfaction from the proud and arrogant westerner who acts as his own judge, jury and executioner. We share the feelings of a tall man who scorns the complexities of big business and bureaucracy. We find momentary comfort in thinking that swift and simple acts of violence can bring lasting justice.

The most popular theory for the glamor of the western film may be that all of the above conventions are merged together in one single story filled with action and set against breathtaking landscapes. No other motion picture ever incorporates such drama, scenery and idealism as is found in the legendary adventures of bandits, lawmen and Indians.

The undefinable attraction of this kind of film existed right from the first days of living pictures. The early moviemakers took advantage of the public's unending appetite for new tales of the frontier. For decades, writers and musicians had advertised the West as a land of lawlessness and adventure.

Fact was mixed with fiction, and each year the exploits were more exaggerated and the truth less evident. Even "Buffalo Bill" Cody in the 1870's had capitalized on the ignorance of the tenderfoots by bringing his Wild West show, starring "Wild Bill" Hickok, to those unable or unwilling to go beyond the borders of Kansas and Missouri. Now for less than the price of an expensive ticket to Cody's show, for less than the cost of the sensationalized dime novels, for just a penny you could see living pictures of "Buffalo Bill," a cattle roundup, or an Indian war party.

In 1901, one man dominated the technical and commercial world of film: Thomas Alva Edison. He was powerful, highly respected, and held the opinion that moving pictures were a passing fancy. He discouraged any individuality in his film producton, choosing instead to emphasize standardization for the purpose of making as much money as possible before the poor and illiterate people, who made up the major portion of the film audience, tired of this trite new toy.

Edison had in his employ a thirty-two years old mechanic who delighted in trying new things. The inquisitive young man had turned his attention to camerawork and had become intrigued with the potential of movies for doing more than merely recording action. He saw in film a great narrative power. Edwin S. Porter was no revolutionist. In many respects he shared his employer's views on the future of film. But, as he convinced Edison, the novelty of story films might prove to be a highly profitable venture. In any event, Edison's competitors in Europe were experimenting with the idea. And so the mechanic was given permission to work on his special project.

The casual Mr. Porter would make a handful of successful story films during his seventeen years in the business and retire in 1915 with a considerable fortune which he would later lose in the stock market crash of 1929. Yet no greater success ever came his way than in the fall of 1903 when he created *The Great Train Robbery*.

3

Although advertised as a Western, the scenes were actually shot near Dover, New Jersey. There were fourteen scenes in all, and depending upon the exhibitor's handling of the 800-foot-film, it took eight-to-ten minutes to project.

The film opened up with an indoor shot of two bandits forcing a telegraph operator to decoy a train into a trap. Except for the superimposed shot of the train through the open window of the artificial set, the scene was typical of the staged actions of the early photoplays and was filmed against a painted background.

Then Porter began to thrill his audience. After the bandits bound and gagged the clerk, the director switched the action of the film to an outside location without using any camera tricks or subtitles. By using logic, he allowed the action to continue with unusual visual smoothness. When the train made its false stop at the water tower, the outlaws sneaked aboard. Porter then cut to an interior shot of the express car where a brave messenger was trying unsuccessfully, to stop the robbers from breaking in and stealing the money. The gunfight, the cold-blooded murder of the messenger, and the use of dynamite to blow open the safe were just a few of the incidents which were shortly to become clichés of the classic western film. What excited audiences in 1903 as well, was the visual novelty of seeing several sets used in one film, dramatic shifts back-and-forth between interior and exterior locations, and the joining together of two actions which seemed to be occurring at the same time.

After the safe was blown open, Porter took the action to the top of the tender of the moving train and proceeded to show two outlaws overpowering the engineer and the fireman, killing the latter and tossing his body off the fast-moving train. Considering the year, one marvels at the impressive camerawork which almost masks the substitution of a dummy for the actor before the body is tossed from the engine.

4

When the locomotive is finally brought to a halt, the bandits force the passengers to turn over their valuables, killing one man who tries to escape. The engine is then uncoupled from the rest of the train, the robbers force the engineer to take them a few miles down the track, then leave the railroad and make their getaway on horseback.

At this point, Porter picked up the tempo of the action. He switched to the telegraph operator being rescued by his daughter and then to a western dance hall where local tough guys are amusing themselves by shooting bullets at the feet of a dude to make him dance. Within seconds, however, the stunned clerk enters the room and announces to the merrymakers that a robbery has been committed. The men immediately grab their rifles and rush outside to form a posse. In the next scene the pursuers surprise the outlaws and a fast-moving, gun-shooting chase ends with the death of all the bandits, which proves that crime does not pay. In the final scene, the outlaw leader, wearing black clothes and a big mustache, points his gun at the audience and shoots. Edison gave the exhibitor the choice of showing that shot at the beginning of the film if the theater owner felt it was a more appropriate place.

If we judge *The Great Train Robbery* by present-day western movies then the film will seem crude, old-fashioned and ineffective. But seen in the light of 1903, Porter had scored a major triumph. We need to remember that studios at that time were really motion-picture factories; that the art of the film had not even been discussed, let alone discovered; and that the shabbiness of the screenings discouraged any self-respecting individual from going to or appearing in the cheap photoplays. Furthermore, *The Great Train Robbery* was extremely topical. The infamous gang, The Wild Bunch, had made their last raid on July 3, 1901, robbing a train belonging to the Great Northern Railroad. After that, Butch Cassidy and the

Sundance Kid came East with their girl friend, Etta Place. Things had gotten too warm for them in the West. They spent some time in New York City and in March 1902, set sail to rob banks in South America. A member of their former outlaw group decided he wanted to join them, but he needed money. Kid Curry, on July 7, 1903, rode from his hideout near Parachute, Colorado, to rob a train and died in the attempt. Porter's film was released two months later.

The Great Train Robbery also serves as a useful illustration of the lawless conditions existing in the infant industry itself. The courts had ruled that a film maker could not copyright his movies since they were not a recognized art form. Taking advantage of this situation, many a fly-by-night film company capitalized on Porter's popular movie by pirating a copy of the original negative, making minor changes in the movie, and selling "duped" prints at reduced prices. Perhaps the boldest case was by an immigrant Polish peddler recently turned film manufacturer, Sigmund "Pop" Lubin. His Philadelphia firm only changed the calendar in the opening scene before releasing the exact same film as the Porter movie.

Antics like this so aroused Edison's anger that he soon instructed his attorneys to bring legal action against his growing list of competitors. Besides, he was just realizing that movies were no fad. The films were not copyrighted, but the cameras and the projectors were, and motion pictures were nothing without the equipment. Thus the great Patents War began. Moving swiftly, Edison's legal force began putting dozens of film companies out of business. "Pop" Lubin, for example, panicked. Having "duped" many a picture and broken more than his share of the patent laws, Lubin cashed in his equipment and retreated to Europe—at least until Edison simmered down. By 1908, more than a hundred firms were gone.

Not everyone fled before the powerful man's wrath. Some took up arms against the great industrialist, and they fought with as much violence and gunplay as ever was seen in a gangland movie. One such combatent was Colonel William Selig, a former Chicago minstrel show manager who had gone into film manufacturing by plagiarizing the Lumière Brothers' equipment. (The Frenchmen had never patented their designs because they felt that by swearing their employees to secrecy the film plans were safe.) Realizing the enormous popularity of western films, Selig decided to specialize in making them, but he needed protection from Edison's power. His Chicago company was not far enough west. Reports came to him about the beauty of California. Not only could a film maker, in case of legal trouble, take a speedy car trip a mere hundred miles south to the Mexican border, but the excellent weather conditions were ideal for outdoor shooting.

Thus, in the summer of 1907, Selig sent his outstanding director, Francis Boggs, to Los Angeles with a small company of players. They set up a makeshift studio in what was formerly a Chinese laundry and then proceeded to make western movies. Some of their first attempts were titled *The Girl from Montana*, *His First Ride* and *The Bandit King*. Boggs made all three of them in less than a month.

These were, for the most part, typical story films of the time. All were one-reelers emphasizing action, while the plot allowed the just to destroy the wicked. Heroes were saints; villains, sinners. Women and love almost never entered into the action, unless a good reason for killing someone was needed. However, *The Girl from Montana* was unusual for its day. Here the most important character is a cowgirl who rescues her lover from bandits intent on hanging him. In the grand tradition of the legendary West, the heroine gallops by the necktie party and shoots the rope off her boyfriend's neck. It was quite a lot of excitement for less than fifty feet of film.

Unfortunately, Boggs never lived long enough to enjoy his studio's success. One day in the late summer of 1910, while filming a new story, the pioneer director was shot and killed for no apparent reason by a part-time actor who had suddenly

7

gone crazy. Selig was also wounded in the gunfight, but recovered and the following year went on to build the grandest studio of the day. Such were the rewards of western movies.

Others came to California for the same reasons as Selig, but particularly to take advantage of the authentic frontier setting. Among them was the first great cowboy star in the history of moving pictures: G. M. Anderson, better known as "Broncho Billy."

From 1908 to 1914, Mr. Anderson was known as the "King of the cowboys," which wasn't a bad feat for a man who was an average rider, used stunt men for his sensational scenes, and admitted being a poor marksman. He was also rather heavy-set and could hardly be described as a dashing figure. But no other cowboy character appeared so frequently at the local theaters. By the time Broncho Billy was finished, he had established many of the precedents that were to become part of the western movie tradition.

G. M. Anderson, born Max Aaronson in 1882, spent his formative years in Little Rock, Arkansas. Before he entered motion pictures he had an undistinguished career as a salesman, vaudevillian, and an artist's model. Then one day he was interviewed by Edwin S. Porter for a part in *The Great Train Robbery*. When asked if he could ride, the beefy man smirked and bragged that he had been raised on a horse. So Porter gave him a bit-part as one of the bandits. Legend has it that during one of the riding scenes, the director couldn't locate Mr. Aaronson, and not wanting to lose the valuable sunlight, shot the episode without him. Later that evening Porter found the answer to his mystery. It seems that on the way to the location Max Anderson had been thrown by his horse and gotten so disgusted that he returned the mount to the stables, and took the next train back to New York City. Afterwards he only worked in the bandits' horseless scenes. And that's how some people describe the beginning of a famous cowboy's career.

8

In 1904, G. M. Anderson, as he now referred to himself, moved from Edison studios to Vitagraph pictures. Here he had a chance to become a director and stayed with the firm for two years. But he wanted more work and in 1906 decided to try his luck and go to work for Colonel Selig. It was while he was in Chicago that year that Anderson renewed his friendship with George K. Spoor, a theatrical booking agent and brother-in-law of Billy Sunday, the internationally known evangelist. Max and George agreed that there was a fortune to be made in motion pictures, and eventually formed a partnership in February 1907: the Essanay Film Company (S and A representing Spoor and Anderson). This was the same outfit that years later could brag that it had helped develop such great personalities as Gloria Swanson, Wallace Beery and Charles Chaplin.

Anderson closely watched Selig's cowboy and Indian films being made on the West Coast. He decided they were such fun that Essanay should make a couple itself. By the spring of 1908, Anderson had set up a small film operation in Niles, California, more than four hundred miles north of Los Angeles.

No one has been able to establish the exact date when the Broncho Billy idea came to the stocky producer-director. Somehow he read Peter Kyne's sentimental account of an outlaw who turns good when he decides to save a sick child instead of escaping from his pursuers. The story was titled *Broncho Billy and the Baby.* Having chosen to make it into a movie, Anderson had trouble casting the main character Pressed for time, he decided to play the part himself. The rest is film history. Overnight, Broncho Billy became a sensation.

For the next six years, Anderson wrote, starred in and directed more than 375 movies built around the character of this cowboy hero. Once a week, shooting from a skimpy script and with a budget of about $800 for each film, Anderson presented the dramatic image of the heroic westerner—a strong individualist who lived by his own laws, a tough man with saintly virtues. Broncho Billy's costume was almost always the same: a big Stetson hat, a dark wide-open shirt with a large white bandanna, wide gloves, fancy corduroy chaps and boots, and two guns. But his character roles weren't as consistent. With so many movies to turn out, Anderson didn't concern himself with Billy's past. In one film, Broncho was part of an outlaw's gang; in another, a medical man; in still another, an alcoholic who later reforms. In one picture, Broncho Billy even got killed. The next week he was back fighting friend and foe alike. Many of Billy's mannerisms remain trademarks of western films today, particularly his shyness with women and his willingness to sacrifice his welfare for the sake of others. Then, too, Billy rode a special horse and almost never kissed the heroines. Years later, Anderson explained the philosophy of his Broncho Billy movies, "We never played our pictures for the physical. We played them for laughs or action."

Gilbert Max Anderson retired from films in 1916. The kind of one- and two-reelers he had been making was going out of style, and his strong but simple little stories were being replaced by a new kind of Western that had more than just an authentic frontier setting.

RESPECTABILITY

As the Western grew in popularity, men like Porter, Selig and Anderson seemed to stand still. Each in his own way had laid the foundation for the work that was to follow. But none of them seemed very much concerned with the art of the film itself.

There was one man, however, whose only concern was the art of the film. He dreamed that one day the movies would become a universal language and act as the guiding force in ending the differences among men. The dreamer was David Wark Griffith, and no artist ever did more to develop the ability of moving pictures to express man's thoughts.

Griffith came reluctantly to the movies. He was a proud Southerner, born in Kentucky on January 23, 1875, committed to the theater, and hoped someday to become a great poet. Like most stage people of that era, Griffith shared Edison's views that living pictures were not to be taken seriously. But in 1907, when theatrical jobs were scarce, he learned that Edison's studio was paying five dollars a day for actors and three times as much for a good script. He decided to try his luck. Griffith brought a screenplay to Edwin S. Porter, who rejected it and at the same time offered the young man a chance to act in his new film. The money was too tempting to refuse, and Griffith took the part of a rugged father who heroically saves his daughter from an eagle in *Rescued from an Eagle's Nest*. Although these were the days when the studios never advertised the name of their players (mostly to avoid increases in salaries), the cautious actor gave his name to the payroll office as "Lawrence" Griffith. He was taking no chance of endangering his stage career. It wasn't until 1914 that he finally gave his proper name to the movie world.

In the meantime, Griffith decided that while he was in motion pictures, he might as well do everything he could to elevate its respectability. There was much that needed changing, and he pondered where he should begin. In 1908, he considered his options: he could either become a roving performer, writer, and director or seek steady employment from one company. He decided on steady work. Next was the problem of which studio to choose. Edison was way up in the Bronx and didn't offer much for the creative artist. Vitagraph was too far out in Brooklyn, Essanay was just getting started in Chicago, and Selig was heading further west. Biograph was in New York City and close to Broadway. So Biograph got the nod.

For the next six years, Griffith, along with an exceptional cameraman named Billy Bitzer, prepared himself to revolutionize the motion picture industry. When he had finished, the movies were a recognized art form. For him, the western film proved to be a wonderful chance to develop new editing techniques, particularly since Griffith was so fascinated with the elements of suspense and storytelling. Given the by-now basic conventions of the good and the bad characters clashing head on, Griffith delighted in presenting the conflict in epic proportions, and then finishing the story with an exciting chase. By

12

intercutting parts of events that were occurring at the same time and then reducing the length of the shots as the climax approached, Griffith, through these exciting chase episodes, involved the audience in the story in a way it had never experienced before.

Those early one- and two-reelers provided Griffith with invaluable opportunities and experiences. They gave him among other things practice in bringing living history to people all over the world. In his western movies like *The Massacre* (1912) and *The Battle at Elderbush Gulch* (1913), Griffith presented astonishing scenes of cowboys, Indians, and soldiers engaged in breathtaking battles. He was superb in the handling of crowd scenes, and few directors today are able to improve on those mob sequences of long ago.

Griffith was also one of the few directors of the period to elevate the stature of the Indian. For the most part the people who made motion pictures were poorly educated and knew very little about history, let alone about the development of the American West. When they made a cowboy and Indian film, their primary sources were the newspapers, magazines, and cheap dime novels which were filled with distorted and vulgar accounts of savage Indians impeding the progress of civilized man. The movies showed Indians, therefore, as simple and barbaric villains who needed destroying so that the West could be made safe for the pioneers. Griffith often presented a fairer view of the western struggle, based somewhat on his love for James Fenimore Cooper's Leatherstocking novels, which romanticized the noble Redman. It was not uncommon in Griffith's cowboy films to note a touch of admiration for the bravery and fighting ability of an Indian unsuccessfully protecting his home, which was unfairly being taken from him.

Almost as important to film history as Griffith and just as much an innovator in these formative years was Thomas H. Ince, who led the industry in systematizing the production of motion pictures. He did not have the enduring or artistic power of a Griffith, but he was a far better businessman. His great success came within a period of six years, but his methods have remained in the industry and were the guiding principles behind the operating standards of the giant studios like Metro-Goldwyn-Mayer and Twentieth Century-Fox.

Born the same year as Max Anderson, Ince followed in the footsteps of his stage parents. Once, in 1903, when he was traveling around the United States in various plays, Ince developed a strong friendship with a promising actor named William Surrey Hart. Years later the two men were reunited and proceded to make the great Westerns of their time. We will come back to them in the next chapter.

Like Anderson and Griffith, Ince drifted into movies because stage work was scarce. But unlike his contemporaries, the short and unattractive actor had no illusions about his future before the camera. Recognizing that he wasn't star material and not willing to settle for bit-parts, he decided to try his luck as a producer-director.

In 1910, he went to work for an outlaw firm called IMP (The Independent Motion Picture Company) which made a habit of boldly antagonizing the big studios like Edison and Biograph. One time IMP stole Biograph's star player, Mary Pickford, and so angered the Patents people that Ince and his troupe had to spend six months in Cuba making movies in order to stay in business.

The new director endured these wild sprees for about fourteen months, learning what he could about film directing and production. But he was getting restless. For almost three years now the major patent owners had been operating as a monopoly which came to be known as the Trust, and it seemed hard for anyone to defeat them. Besides, Ince felt that's where the big money was to be made. One day in 1911, he was called into the office of Adam Kessel, a leading member of the Trust, to discuss a possible job. Ince was a shrewd and cocky businessman and wanted to take no chances with this excellent break. To impress Kessel with a young man's success, Tom borrowed a big diamond ring to wear on his finger. All during the meeting he kept gesturing with his hands. Before Kessel realized what had happened he had hired the diamond-flashing director for ninety dollars more a week than IMP was paying him. Incidents like this only encouraged Ince's already well-established ego.

Within months, Thomas Ince was in Los Angeles taking charge of the Trust's western movies. Charles O. Bauman, Kessel's partner, came to California to help the new producer-director get started. The two men became interested in a group called The Miller Brothers 101 Ranch, a traveling Wild West company that was spending the winters in California. Ince favored the idea of making pictures with a stock company consisting of real cowboys and Indians, along with authentic costumes and props. In addition to all that, this group had trick riders and horses. Bauman agreed to lease the entire show for the winter. Before he could give much further help to Ince, he was called back East where new motion picture wars were getting underway. This left Ince alone on the coast and ready to try movie making his way.

It soon became evident that Ince preferred supervising the entire project rather than just coaching the actors and crew as directors did in those days. It also became evident that he didn't approve of the way that people like Griffith, Porter, and Anderson made pictures. They put too much power in the hands of the director, and he wanted that power for himself. They also preferred to work with simple scripts, improvising as much as possible while doing the actual filming. This was not only time-consuming but costly. Ince was certain he could do better. And so he set about to establish new procedures. He justified his changes on the grounds that he would save money at the studio and make money at the box-office. Movies, he argued, were a business and a strong, tight organization was good business practice. The Ince reforms were to have everything carefully planned, budgeted and executed according to *his* pre-determined ideas and estimates. He developed shooting scripts which detailed each aspect of the story according to the cast and the cost factors. He insisted on shooting schedules which told everyone where to be, when to be there, and what to do while they were there. No one was allowed to deviate from the schedule.

These methods resulted in Westerns which all bore the ideas of Thomas Ince. They were characterized by a style of melodrama which only presented those scenes and players that moved the plot briskly to its conclusion. Almost always the main characters were tough, humorless men usually found in saloons, whose sheer strength and saintly ways made them victorious in a cruel and dangerous world. Each film contained a harsh, realistic setting and was filled with authentic cowboys and Indians who performed exciting and spectacular feats. Sometimes Ince would extend the film an extra reel if he had some good shots of massive battle scenes between the settlers and the redskins. To Ince's credit, he presented the problems of the American West with integrity and courage. For some critics, he presented his stories too realistically, tending to overemphasize the tragic elements. A two-reeler like *Past Redemption,* in 1913, is one example of this. A renegade and his daughter, Ann Little, made a living by selling alcohol to the Indians. But a new preacher in town successfully argued against the evil influences of whiskey and was responsible for the soldiers' attacking the outlaws' headquarters and killing Ann's father. During the gunfight, she kills an Indian to discredit the cavalry and then escapes to kill the preacher. But Ann is caught before she gets her revenge, and by some strange twist of justice is turned over to the minister to be reformed. Eventually the two fall in love, but the hypocritical community won't forgive her for her past deeds, and Ann feels that she is a threat to her lover's future. One night she slips away to commit suicide in the desert. Stories like this made Ince a very popular producer with certain audiences.

In spite of his efforts and themes in 1913, Ince was not in the mainstream of the movie world. The year before, Adolph Zukor had started a company called Famous Players in Famous Plays (later to become Paramount Pictures) in which he brought further respectability to movies. Now well-known actors were eager to appear in movies, and the conservative middle-class audience began to come regularly to newly-built movie palaces to see the elegant films. At this time, foreign film companies were producing four and five reel movies of spectacular events which offered American film producers their first serious competition from abroad. The twelve-minute moviemakers were in trouble.

These pressures for feature films, the war going on in the film industry, and the desire to see famous actors in popular stage plays all influenced the stature of the western film. Those pressures also gave the motion picture world one of its most popular directors: Cecil B. De Mille.

It all came about because Jesse Lasky was going broke. This enterprising individual had drifted from one form of entertainment to another: cornet player, booking agent, vaudevillian and nightclub producer. But in 1913, he needed money —and a fresh start. His brother-in-law was Samuel Goldfish (later Goldwyn), a glove manufacturer who felt that the emerging war in Europe would ruin his business. Sam, however, was an optimist. His legal companion, Arthur Friend, had convinced him that there was a fortune to be made in film production. The three men talked it over and decided that the time was right to form the Jesse L. Lasky Feature Player Company. Jesse wanted William De Mille to take charge of the actual producing operation of the firm, but he declined. So Lasky offered the post to Bill's younger brother, who at the time was thinking of joining the Mexican revolution.

Each of the three men was to invest five thousand dollars as a starting stake in the company. (Cecil B. De Mille went to

Bill and asked for a loan, but the older brother decided instead to put the money aside in case C. B. needed help when the project failed.) De Mille found his share elsewhere. Lasky also offered stage star Dustin Farnum a quarter share in the new corporation if Farnum would star in the company's first film. Dustin agreed.

By the time the company was ready to begin filming, Cecil B. De Mille decided he ought to learn something about the production end of film making. A visit was arranged to Edison's old Bronx studio. In his book "Autobiography" De Mille described what that experience was like:

> I watched the director and the camerman set up the camera and point toward a stone wall alongside a road. The director called for action. The cameraman cranked. A girl emerged from the hedge, climbed the wall, and ran down the road. A man met her, stopped her, and they talked, in pantomime of course, with much emotive gesticulation.

Having completed his visit, De Mille reported to Lasky that he was all set to start.

The stage play chosen as the first film was Edwin Milton Royle's successful Western *The Squaw Man* and cost the Lasky company $15,000 to own. The romantic story told about Captain James Wynngate, an Englishman, who after quarreling with his parents changes his name to Jim Carson and runs away to the American West. There he is rescued from death by a lovely Indian maiden whom he decides to marry. Soon afterwards, he learns that his parents have died and he has become a nobleman with a large estate. The Indian squaw realizes that she stands in the way of her husband's future and forsakes both him and their child to commit suicide in the mountains. (As you can see, women were expendable in the Old West.)

18

The plan was to make the movie in New Jersey because that's where most of the Westerns were still being shot. But De Mille wanted to go into Indian country. Lasky remembered that he had once seen some real Indians in Flagstaff, Arizona, and it was decided to make *The Squaw Man* there. Then Farnum got upset. He wasn't going to work for stock options if he had to move away from New York. He didn't have *that* much confidence in the new company. Lasky Feature pictures faced its first disaster by getting Mrs. Lasky's relatives to buy Farnum's five thousand dollar share of the firm. If the actor had waited eight years to cash in his stocks, he would have gotten close to two million dollars.

That problem settled, general manager De Mille, director Oscar Apfel, cameraman Alfred Gandolifi, and several leading players headed toward Flagstaff. Along the way, they wrote the screenplay. But when the group arrived at their destination, they realized that Flagstaff, Arizona, did not suit their needs. Rather than rewrite the script, which would have been the sensible thing to do, De Mille sent the following telegram to Lasky:

FLAGSTAFF NO GOOD FOR OUR PURPOSES STOP HAVE
PROCEEDED TO CALIFORNIA STOP WANT AUTHORITY
TO RENT BARN IN PLACE CALLED HOLLYWOOD FOR
SEVENTY-FIVE DOLLARS A MONTH STOP REGARDS TO
SAM.

The actual filming began on December 29, 1913, and the best break the new crew got was from the weather. The sun shone almost every day of the filming. But it didn't take long before someone on the set, presumably from the Trust, began to disrupt production by destroying the developed film. De Mille had no other choice but to work and sleep near the valuable celluloid. The opposition had even fired a shot at him. De Mille often referred to his unknown assailant as his first movie critic.

Eventually the movie was completed and ready for a full screening. Lasky came West to attend the performance and everyone waited in the darkened theater as the movie began. Disaster! The film wiggled, slipped, flickered and fell off the projector. The owners were terrified. Not only did everything they had depend upon the picture's success, but Goldfish had already sold the "state's rights." (State's rights meant that a distributor obtained exclusive permission to arrange the screening of a movie in a given state.) Lasky was frantic. No one seemed to know what to do. Finally they agreed there was only one man who could help them, and he worked for the very group that was against them: Pop Lubin. They had no choice but to go to him. If they didn't, it meant not only bankruptcy but also jail. They had already used the state's rights money.

Lubin listened patiently as Lasky and De Mille told their sad story. Then he looked at the film they had brought with them. After a while Lubin turned to them with a big grin on his face. Nothing was wrong with the valuable print. In an effort to save money C. B. De Mille had bought a used sprocket puncher made in England. American projectors ran on a different ratio of sprockets per minute. All that was necessary was to repunch the sprocket holes to make *The Squaw Man* the first important feature film made in Hollywood, and the beginning of a new trend in Westerns.

The first cowboy star: Broncho Billy Anderson. (ESSANAY)

Two bandits forcing a telegraph operator to decoy a train into a trap in
Edwin Porter's *The Great Train Robbery* (Edison, 1903).

W. S. Hart and "Fritz." So passionate was the star's love for animals that when he directed a film he would fire any actor who mistreated a horse.

(*left*) Dustin Farnum and Red Wing in a scene from Hollywood's first full-length cowboy film *The Squaw Man* (1913). This particular shot illustrates the melodrama and staginess of the early Westerns.

Hoot Gibson, the cowboy who mixed humor and action, appears here with Marion Hircon. The cowboy's empty gun holster was a familiar device in Gibson movies, proving that a man could succeed without violence, at least, until the last reel.

right) Tom Mix and "Tony." Over a period of twenty-five years there were actually five horses named Tony.

Ken Maynard with "Tarzan." The horse had bad vision, and often Maynard used doubles for his mount in order to avoid riding straight into a tree.

Dustin Farnum (right) in Cecil B. De Mille's *The Virginian* (1914). This was the forerunner of films about the strong but silent cowboy who kills the villain and wins the girl.　(THE BETTMANN ARCHIVE)

A scene from W. S. Hart's final and epic film, *Tumbleweeds* (1925). The real "Bat" Masterson had once described Hart as the major spokesman of the nineteenth-century cowboy. In this movie, with Barbara Bedford, Hart presented the last realistic scenes of the great land rushes.

(UNITED ARTISTS)

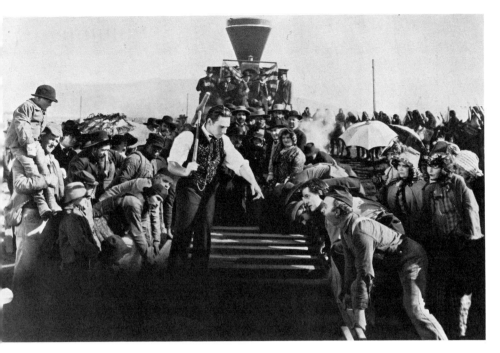

The Iron Horse (1924). Ford achieved his best effects when he recreated the westward movement through actual events rather than following the film's weak love story. Here we see a typical scene depicting the building of the railroad.   (BETTMANN/SPRINGER FILM ARCHIVE)

Gary Cooper (left) and Walter Huston appear in the first sound version of *The Virginian* (1929). The static quality of this shot illustrates the awkwardness of the early talkies.   (BETTMANN/SPRINGER FILM ARCHIVE)

THE VIRGINIAN'S CODE

The war between the Trust and the Independents came to a climax in 1914. When it was over, the old order was dead and the outlaw companies were in control for the first time. This turnabout had far-reaching effects for western movies.

The main event was between the General Film Company, the Trust's distributing agency, and its New York Film Rental group, run by William Fox. Since 1912, the unpredictable and uncontrollable Fox, well-known for his violent temper, had hammered away at the oppressive policies of the Patents people. No matter what they did to him—financially, emotionally or socially—the bold and seemingly indestructible movie pioneer stood his ground against the mammoth organization. The General Film Company became obsessed with one idea: destroy Fox. They tried and failed. They reasoned that the next best thing to do was to give him what he asked for . . . at least, within reason. Finally, a settlement was arranged and they thought the matter was ended. But Fox fooled them. He took the terms of the settlement to court as evidence in an anti-trust suit against the Patents companies.

All this trouble and bad publicity so preoccupied the Trust that it had no time to worry about its competitors. For the first time in motion picture history the Independents were left alone, and it had a strange effect on them. Instead of uniting to strengthen their position, the competitive studios took advantage of the situation to further their own ambitions.

Adolph Zukor was one Independent who watched the squabbling and the chaos with a keen eye for business. His ideas about famous actors and longer films had caught on so well that everywhere producers were paying fantastic salaries for stars and well-known directors.

Zukor was looking for a new opportunity when W. W. Hodkinson approached him with a revolutionary idea. The men agreed that financial success in the movie industry rested on the rental and exhibition of movies. They further agreed that the present system of state's rights distribution was too costly and too long a process. Hodkinson proposed to start a new national agency which would rent pictures to the theater owners on a "block-booking" basis. The exhibitors would rent, sight unseen, blocks of movies—13, 26, 52 or 104 a year. The choices would be made on the basis of the producer's name, the date the picture was released, the title of the movie and the name of the star. Each theater, or chain of theaters, could purchase a franchise which might run as long as five or ten years. (No exhibitor at the time worried that his theater would have to show a film that he hadn't first seen himself or that the practice of block booking would force him to rent a number of bad movies just to get a single good one.)

Hodkinson convinced the owner of Famous Players in Famous Plays to go along with the plan. Next they approached Jesse Lasky. Because of *The Squaw Man*, the Lasky-Goldfish-De Mille combination had developed a large stock company to turn out at least thirty films a year. And they were buying screen rights to as many popular plays as were available. (An important reason for this was that in the silent days of movies, once screen rights were purchased, the property belonged to the studio for life. Studios could then make the same film as often as they wanted. This unfair practice toward authors was stopped with the coming of sound.) Hodkinson's new organization offered Lasky pictures a chance to make more money because of better distribution. Lasky joined. A few more producers were added to the list and the new agency was ready to begin.

Legend has it that one day on the way to work, Hodkinson passed an impressive apartment building with an attractive title. He decided to use it for his new venture and thus Paramount Pictures Corporation was named.

Because of these exciting and dramatic events, Cecil B. De Mille's new film, the first one of seventy that he directed on his own, was not released until September of 1914. But it was worth waiting for.

The Virginian, once a best-selling book and successful play, became a milestone in the history of western movies. The pictorial work was fine, the acting commendable. But the original story contained the classic ingredients that almost all Western actors and directors were to imitate for the next forty years. The setting was Medicine Bow, Wyoming, during the days when cattlemen held the western spotlight. The hero was a cowboy known only as the Virginian. We first meet him in a saloon poker game where one of his bunkhouse companions accuses him of cheating. The matter is quickly settled by the Virginian's fast draw, and Trampas, his opponent, has to apologize, and he becomes the lifelong enemy of the hero.

Into the cowboy's life comes pretty Molly Wood, a schoolteacher from Vermont. The two meet, and the tall, bashful and awkward wrangler vows to himself that he is going to marry that Eastern girl. One night, at a barbecue, Molly appears to reject the Virginian's unpolished ways. His first response is to get drunk. Determined to win her love, the cowboy, who had never gone beyond the sixth grade, decides to learn how to read. This makes a very favorable impression not only on Molly but also on the wrangler's boss, Judge Henry. To indicate his pleasure, the judge puts the ranchhand in charge of a group of men, including Trampas, assigned to escort a herd of steers to market.

30

On the way back to the ranch, the villain tries to discredit the Virginian by plotting with the men to quit their jobs and go prospecting for gold. But the hero's humor and quick-thinking turn the wranglers against the scheme, and everyone returns to work. The clever cowboy is rewarded by being made foreman of the ranch. He decides to keep Trampas on the payroll where he can be watched.

Things seem to be going well until the following spring, when the hero runs into an Indian ambush. Although badly wounded, the Virginian escapes, but is unable to make it back to the ranch. Fortunately, Molly finds him in time and nurses him back to health. During these peaceful days the two realize they love each other, and Molly agrees to marry him.

When the happy and healthy foreman returns to his job, he finds Trampas missing. At the same time, he learns that a band of cattle rustlers is working the range. The ranchers form a posse, placing the Virginian in charge. After a long and tiring search, two of the rustlers are captured; one of them is the hero's best friend. The cowboy feels bad but since his friend broke the law, he must pay the penalty. Because the town courts are run by crooked politicians, the posse decides to hang the two men then and there. The Virginian can do nothing but watch as frontier justice is done. But the hero promises vengeance on Trampas, who is revealed to be the leader of the rustlers.

At first, Molly is shocked at the news of the hanging, but Judge Henry convinces her that things are done differently in the Wild West. Here the lawlessness of the times demands severe measures and strong men to enforce them. Molly and the Virginian are reconciled.

The day before their wedding the happy couple ride to town to make last minute preparations. On the way they encounter Trampas, but Molly stops her fiancé from taking any immediate action. By the time they reach Medicine Bow, however, Trampas has made it known that if the Virginian is not out of town by sunset, he will kill him. Molly pleads with her lover not to face his opponent. She threatens to forsake him unless he leaves with her now and avoids bloodshed. Her threats mean nothing to the man of honor. He has no other choice.

At dusk the two men face each other. Trampas draws his gun and fires first, missing. Then the Virginian shoots . . . and the feud is finally finished. When the victor returns, Molly realizes that she loves this cowboy because she respects him. She knows now that his way is right. The next day they get married and ride off into the hills.

The creator of these classic situations was Owen Wister, a personal friend of President Theodore Roosevelt, and a man who loved the romance of the sagebrush cowboys. Like many a tenderfoot, Wister regarded the cowhand as the last direct descendant of King Arthur's legendary knights. The difference between Wister and lesser Eastern romantics was that he gave his hero a human life, whereas the others gave him a gun and made him a glorified killer. For people unfamiliar with the West, the Virginian came to symbolize the best of the unseen cowboy. He appeared gallant as well as heroic, and he had weaknesses. He got drunk when things didn't go his way, he played practical jokes, didn't have much formal education, and had his problems with women. At the same time, he had unusual strength, wit, an exceptional understanding of human nature and good common sense. He remained calm in the face of danger, and whenever possible, he chose to be kind and gentle. Yet neither his friends nor his foes mistook his soft-talking style for weakness. They knew he lived by an inflexible moral code, and no one or nothing could divert him from justice. And they knew that when he had to, the Virginian became a two-fisted and deadly gunfighter. He was the best the West had created.

Even if there wasn't a bit of truth to this cowboy legend, it was a marvelous story filled with romance and adventure. People of all ages never seemed to tire of the tale. For De Mille it was a perfect venture. He prided himself on being both a great showman and a practical film maker. He truly believed that his job was to give the public what it wanted, only more magnificent than they expected. And for over forty years, his uncanny ability to change with the times enabled him to become one of Hollywood's most successful directors. Years later, Bob Hope would say of the great popularizer, "Cecil B. De Mille is indeed 'Mr. Motion Picture.' His films have brought something new to theaters. They call them customers."

Even in his first solo film, De Mille worked hard to satisfy his audience, taking twice as long as his associates to make one movie. His interest was in turning the Wister story into a lavish and visual spectacular. Lasky's previous releases had minimized the number of interior shots in favor of the more accessible (and therefore inexpensive) outdoor locations. De Mille felt that his movie should have greater pictorial flexibility. So he imported one of Broadway's best stage men and became the first director to have a set designer construct buildings and rooms to give more variety to the art of the story film. *The Virginian* was ballyhooed as a movie in five parts with four hundred scenes. He proved it when audiences waited breathlessly for the projectionist to change the reels and show the next part.

Another De Mille pre-occupation during this movie was the creative use of lights. Prior to his arrival on the West Coast, producers and directors measured the photographic success of a movie by the clarity of the picture. De Mille felt that there was more to photography than this. He set out to prove his point. He experimented, for example, in the scene where the two captured cattle rustlers are hanged. To show the actual hanging seemed too horrifying for the squeamish viewers of the day. Consequently, lights were placed in back and to the side of the men, and De Mille ordered his camera-man to photograph the shadows on the ground of the two men receiving their sentence. (That dramatic shot has been imitated so often in motion pictures that it has become a film cliché.) During other moments in the film, the director used subdued lights to create dramatic and tender moods. The story is often told that when Goldfish saw the finished version of the movie, he wired Lasky and asked how he was to rent a film to exhibitors when the lighting was so poor that half the time you couldn't even see the actor's features. (Griffith ran into a similar type of objection at Biograph when he was doing his experimental work with close-ups. The producer was angry because Griffith was paying a whole actor but only using parts of him.) Jesse presented the telegram to Cecil. He considered it and then said, "Tell him it's Rembrandt lighting." When Sam got the answer he was delighted, and raised the price of the film rental.

If *The Squaw Man* convinced Dustin Farnum to remain a movie actor, *The Virginian* made him a star. It also convinced Selig to capitalize on the Farnum name and hire Dustin's brother and stage star, William, to star in Rex Beach's exciting action tale, *The Spoilers.* Eventually this splended fighting story was remade several times because of the classic and gripping situations dealing with the lawlessness of the Yukon during the great gold rush, pictured as a claim jumper's paradise. But in 1915, it was the last thrilling sequence of the movie which made film history and turned Bill Farnum into one of the great early cowboy stars. Bill played the hero and Tom Santschi played the villain, and they met in the final reel for the showdown. Both actors agreed to make the fight as realistic as possible, with no phony punches. What followed was so brutal that both men spent weeks in the hospital recovering from probably the wildest fight in cowboy movies. But *The Spoilers* was a hit. Bill Farnum's starring days came to an end in 1929 when his brother died and the stock market crash forced him into temporary retirement. When movies began to speak he returned to the screen, but never again reached the heights of his silent days.

The attack on the encircled pioneers from James Cruze's *The Covered Wagon*. (Note the studio's tent city in the upper left.) (1923).

Raoul Walsh's *In Old Arizona* (1929) proved that the old Cisco Kid stories of the silent era made excellent talking films. Here we see Conchita Montenegro trying her tricks on Warner Baxter (Cisco) and Edmund Lowe.

(*left*) Sheriff Pat Garrett (Wallace Beery) shoots William Bonney (Johnny Mack Brown) while Clair (Kay Johnson) looks on in King Vidor's *Billy the Kid* (1930).

(BETTMANN/SPRINGER FILM ARCHIVE)

Richard Dix and Irene Dunne as the adventurous Cravats who helped settle Oklahoma in Wesley Ruggles' *Cimarron* (1931).

(BETTMANN/SPRINGER FILM ARCHIVE)

Destry (James Stewart) breaks up a fight between Frenchy (Marlene Dietrich) on the right and Lily Belle Callahan (Una Merkel) on the left. It seems as if both feel strongly about the lawmen in George Marshall's *Destry Rides Again* (1939).　(BETTMANN/SPRINGER FILM ARCHIVE)

Young and old have cheered the exploits of Hopalong Cassidy (William Boyd) and his horse "Topper" for more than thirty years.

John Ford's first use of the lovely Monument Valley came in *Stagecoach* (1939). (UNITED ARTISTS)

The passengers of John Ford's *Stagecoach* (1939) discover, during a meal-time break, that they are in the midst of an Indian uprising. From left to right: Donald Meek, John Wayne, Claire Trevor, Andy Devine, George Bancroft, Louise Platt, Tim Holt, John Carradine, Berton Churchill, Chris Martin, and Thomas Mitchell. (UNITED ARTISTS)

Gene Autry (*left*) ushered in a new era of Westerns, de-emphasizing action and concentrating on comedy, music and a star's personality. Soon after Gene Autry successfully developed the idea of the singing cowboy, along came a finer rider and better singer: Roy Rogers with his horse "Trigger."

THE REAL COWBOY

In spite of De Mille's success and the popularity of such actors as the Farnums, western movies were not very popular in 1914. They seemed to have worn out the audience's patience with the same old formulas. Then came William Surrey Hart.

Unlike his predecessors, the great star of the silent days of motion pictures had learned about the West firsthand. Born in Newburgh, New York, in 1870, Bill traveled for almost fifteen years with his wandering family to Minnesota, Wisconsin and the Dakotas. On June 25, 1876—that memorable day in frontier history when General George Armstrong Custer was killed at the battle of the Little Big Horn—the Harts were living about three hundred miles from the main strength of the Sioux nation. The time even came when the boy would talk to Sioux warriors who had been in the fight only to learn that there had been much confusion and much dust. (Dime novelists later wrote that Custer was the last killed, flashing his saber to the end. Not only did Custer not carry his sword with him to the fight, but the Sioux did not know Custer was there until after the battle. And no one knew who died last.) Hart also learned in his childhood to love and respect the Indian, his ways and his traditions. Unlike many people who moved across the frontier in the last half of the nineteenth century, Hart did not fear the Red Men, nor had he come to trespass on their lands, kill their game, destroy their homes and starve their families to death. Much to Hart's credit, he had the courage throughout his life to re-mind America that his country (which he loved dearly) had soiled its honor by its unforgivable treatment of a courageous minority.

The famous cowboy star in later years counted among his personal associates such popular folk heroes of the day as Wyatt Earp and Bartholomew "Bat" Masterson. Often these self-made legendary peace officers told the naive Hart fan-tastic stories about Dodge City, Deadwood, and Abilene. Naturally, they always added a little to their prowess in the narration. All the same, it gave Hart direct contact with the type of men who helped tame the West. Woven into these glorified accounts were the adventures of infamous men like Doc Holliday, the psychopathic gun-slinger from Georgia; and Billy the Kid, the homicidal runt from New York City.

As a youngster, Hart had two ambitions: to attend West Point and to become a professional actor. No doubt his inter-est in a military career was somewhat related to his many visits to the frontier forts and the countless hours he listened to the soldiers who had fought in the great Indian wars. But Bill was not a serious student, nor had his nomadic travels helped much in giving him a formal education. So this hope of going to West Point soon faded. He did, however, become an important stage performer.

It was during his theatrical days that Hart first acquired a reputation as an authority on the real frontier. It seems that while appearing in the stage version of *The Virginian*, he expressed the view that Wister was a great writer—who else could have taken such nonsense and made it into such a delightful story? The rising actor pointed out that in the real West, no wrangler would hunt down his friend, and no one would have expected him to. Even if he had joined in the search, he would have done so only to throw the posse off the trail. The posse would have expected him to, and no one would have thought less of him for doing it. Even further, if the Virginian did catch up with his friend, he would have done so intentionally. As Hart explained it in his autobiography "My Life East and West": "He would have stepped to his friend's side and said: 'Well gentlemen, I've done my duty and brought you here, but if you hang him, you've got to hang me too! And we ain't neither of us strong for being hung while we've got our guns on.'" Hart went on to remind his audience that cattle rustling was more of a hanging offense in theory than in practice. "The majority of owners didn't hesitate to brand a few, and the minority couldn't be trusted, either."

One day in 1914 he happened to see a cowboy film in a movie theater in Cleveland. Afterwards, in a discussion with the theater owner, Hart learned that this was one of the best Westerns ever shown in Ohio. No one seemed to care that the setting, the acting and the costumes were all phony. According to the great star, he decided then and there that his future was in western films. On his next trip to California that summer, Hart left his touring company of actors and looked up his friend Tom Ince, whom he hadn't seen in eleven years. The manager of the New York Motion Picture Company, the name of the firm owned by Kessel and Bauman, told his former acting companion that he'd love to give him a job, but western movies were dying out. Bill couldn't believe it. After all, Ince still had one more year to go on his contract with the 101 Ranch outfit. Surely the movie company intended to do something with so many available cowboys and Indians. Ince continued to argue that the public didn't care about the tales of the West anymore. He cited the example of the movie he had filmed more than a year before, *Custer's Last Fight*, which was a real spectacular yet never made any money. (Ince with his usual modesty had advertised the picture as "The greatest wild west feature ever made." The producer overlooked the fact that the mediocre movie didn't do much to vary the pattern set by many other two-reelers.) Persisting in his aim of revolutionizing Westerns, however, Bill convinced Ince to let him try a few films.

Hart's first pictures were the run-of-the-mill two-reelers where he played the parts of the bad guys. But he wanted better roles for himself and pleaded with Tom for a chance to work in feature films. So Ince gave him the script of a previously made short film and asked him to expand it. Four days later Hart was back with a full story and got the okay to make his first five-reeler, *The Bargain*. When that was finished, he beefed up another script and made *On the Midnight Stage*. By the end of two months he had finished his assigned work and approached the question of his future. Ince offered him a contract to direct but not star in films. Reluctantly, Bill turned it down. He was forty-three years old, had come West in hope of becoming a great cowboy star and considered the gamble a failure. He took the next train back to New York City and Broadway.

A week passed. Then came the following telegram:

CAN OFFER YOU ONE-TWENTY-FIVE PER WEEK AS A STAR. ONE YEAR CONTRACT. YOU TO DIRECT YOUR OWN PICTURES. WIRE ANSWER. TOM.

Hart was delighted. He wired back his acceptance. Bill might have waited a while if he had known that Ince had released *The Bargain* through Zukor's Famous Players and it had become an overnight sensation. His mistake was in trusting Tom, who, being shrewd and opportunistic, took advantage of their relationship and hired Bill for an incredibly low salary.

By this time, the film wars once more redirected the destiny of western movies. Ince's outfit, The New York Motion Picture Company, distributed its product through Mutual, owned by Ray and Harry Aitken and John R. Freuler. Harry was a speculator; John, a former small-town banker, was not. The men were constantly quarreling. After a disagreement they refused to talk to each other. It was during one of these periods that Aitken went ahead, without his partner's permission, and gave one of their directors, D. W. Griffith, forty thousand dollars of Mutual's money to begin making a film called *The Clansman*, a brilliant but distorted account of the Civil War.

Harry's decision proved more troublesome than even he had imagined. The picture wasn't even half-finished when Griffith came back to his producer requesting another twenty thousand dollars. It was given to him to safeguard the original investment. Freuler was beside himself with anger. Then came additional requests for money and the picture was finally finished with its total cost amounting to $110,000. Released under the title *The Birth of a Nation*, the movie not only became a magnificent film achievement, but it also got Harry Aitken booted out of Mutual.

Undaunted by the chain of events, Aitken contracted Kessel and Bauman, who had Mack Sennett, Tom Ince, and Bill Hart under contract, and before long a new movie organization was created: The Triangle Film Corporation, whose top producers were Ince, Sennett and Griffith. The idea was to take advantage of the public's interest in stars not only by making their own films and distributing them, but also by opening a chain of theaters across the country to show Triangle movies.

Hart's first feature for the new organization, and his fifth for Ince, was called *The Disciple*. Compared to Griffith's latest release, it was made for peanuts. The female lead earned $40 a week. The assistant director was paid $30. The script cost $75. The villain earned $25 per week. The extras were

46

paid $5 a week plus board, with the top hands making as much as $6 and $8 per week. The foreman of the crew received $10. And W. S. Hart—star, director and part-time screenwriter—earned the whopping salary of $125 per week, or about $2,000 less than he deserved. The total film cost about $8,000 and made a small fortune for Tom Ince.

In many respects, Hart already had solidified most of the conventions of his particular brand of Western in *The Disciple*. The plot typified his interest in showing the virtuous triumph over the slick ways of the saloon gamblers. (In this respect, he may have been influenced by Ince's western films, since they were the textbooks for Hart in his early study of editing.) In this particular story, Parson Jim Houston (Hart) comes to Barren Gulch to build a house of God. But shortly thereafter, his pretty but foolish wife runs away with "Doc" Hardy, saloon owner and gambler. Jim blames the Lord for his trouble, forsakes the church, and takes his child Kate with him into the mountains. Then, by a series of events believable only to a true sentimentalist, Kate becomes ill, Mary miraculously returns to her daughter's bedside in what may have been the worst storm in western films up to that time, "Doc" saves the child's life, and Houston reunited with his family returns to his missionary work. As the reader might guess, Hart was particularly fond of scenes in which people were allowed to reform out of love for men, women and later on, horses.

Another typical Hart convention was the authentic appearance of his frontier towns, suggesting the harsh and unglamorous life of the West. In each town there was a saloon (in the real West the cow towns usually had more than fifteen whiskey palaces lined up alongside each other), where rowdies, gamblers and prostitutes waited with liquor and cards to steal the cowpuncher's money. But in Bill's movies, the costumes always seemed more realistic, the barroom brawls more authentic. Illustrative of this point is the opening saloon scene in *The Disciple* where a gunfight takes place between two wranglers. In most movies, you'd expect the bystanders to run away or hide so as not to get wounded. Not in a Hart film. Everyone crowded around and watched. Bill had learned from his father, years before, that when two real cowboys fought, the best thing to do was to stand still. They knew what they were aiming at. You only took cover when amateurs were wielding pistols. Then no one was safe.

Hart also treated women differently in his Westerns. In Wister's *The Virginian*, for example, Molly represented one type of Eastern female who came West and clashed with the cowpuncher's world. She was gentle, refined and gifted with a superior knowledge denied to those living on the frontier. But in *The Disciple*, Mary, possessed with similar virtues, wanted more out of life than getting up at 5 A.M. to make the morning bread and then working throughout the day and night until she fell asleep at 9 P.M. The beautiful woman also wanted love and attention. Like Molly, she appeared childlike compared to the ruggedness of her man, but unlike the Virginian's woman (or those of the early Ince films), Mary became a stronger person as the film continued. She changed, not because of her lover's honor, but because of her better understanding of life itself. In later stories, Hart would make it a point to be even more severe with his motion picture ladies, paying for those he desired, seducing those he couldn't buy, or just leaving town when a civilized woman wanted to tie him down.

Compared to the western movies made before and after Hart's time, his films emphasized the dramatic nature of frontier lives more than the traditional scenes of gunfights, barroom brawls and spectacular battles. In *The Disciple*, for instance, there is only one gunfight, and the cowboy hero leaps onto his horse just once, and then only because he is in a rush to save his child's life. Although an expert rider and an outstanding track star, Hart disliked stunts because he felt they often appeared artificial. He felt tricks should be used only when they came naturally in the melodrama itself.

48

But the best of the conventions was W. S. Hart's portrayal of the strong, silent frontiersman. He once explained that his heroes rarely spoke because the West had made men feel small in comparison to its vastness, and a man only talked when he had something worth saying. But Hart had other ways of showing a man's character and strength. In *The Disciple,* for example, the sheriff goes into Doc's saloon to stop a fight, and just as he is about to close the door the big preacher comes in, and the camera pans slowly to the silent but impressive stranger. Another scene shows some rowdies from the saloon bringing a keg of whiskey to the steps of the newly-erected church to celebrate its opening. The preacher's stern looks are enough to disperse the mob.

This role of a preacher was not the typical Bill Hart character. More often he preferred the part of a good-badman who reformed during the course of the story. In some respects this was a carryover from the tradition of Broncho Billy, whom Hart replaced in 1915 as the number one cowboy star in the world. Hart's badmen shared the characteristics of the traditional outlaws; they drank, gambled, smoked and enjoyed the company of wild women. But they were also unique, considering that they never abused a child, betrayed a friend, or blasphemed against God. They had a strange mixture of gentility and guts.

When Bill's contract with Ince came up for renewal, further trouble developed between the two men. Hart had developed a lasting love for one of the company's ponies, Fritz, and used him in all his movies. Tom knew this and refused to sell the horse to the star, figuring that it was just one more hold on his great box-office attraction. But Bill insisted. A compromise was worked out. If Hart made his next film free, he could have Fritz. It was agreed and although he never regretted it, Hart figured that Fritz had cost him over forty-two thousand dollars.

By 1917, Triangle, because of a number of incredibly bad movies and some dishonest stock manipulation, was nearing the end of its days. Ince left and sought greener pastures. He asked Bill to stay with him. In spite of the many offers being made to the famous star, he agreed to see what Ince could arrange. Tom, without Bill's knowledge or permission, signed a new contract with Zukor. There was a special clause that stated Hart would make sixteen pictures for Famous Player's new subdivision, Artcraft. A month after the deal was concluded, Bill signed his contract with Ince. The shrewd producer had promised his friend that he would have his usual freedom to make his own kind of movie.

Hart quickly learned that this was not true. As soon as he began work at Artcraft, people interfered with his every effort. In desperation he went to Ince, expecting the boss to stop the current meddling. But Tom had no such plans. He insisted that Bill adjust to the new conditions—this from a man who had millions from his friend's sweat. The argument grew and finally Hart had to take his case to court. Although bitter and disillusioned, Hart, being an honorable man, completed his sixteen pictures. (Years later he won his case in court.)

Ince was not Hart's greatest mistake. That came in 1919 when the cowboy's friends—Douglas Fairbanks, Charles Chaplin, D. W. Griffith and Mary Pickford—asked him to join with them in creating a new film company, United Artists. They, like Hart, had suffered at the hands of the producers. Now they decided to go into business for themselves. But a disagreement arose on the manner in which the new company was to be financed. They wanted to use their own money. Hart didn't. So he decided against the deal. It was the chance of a lifetime and he missed out.

After that, he became an independent producer, releasing his movies through Artcraft. But his popularity was decreasing at the box-office. The public was growing tired of the same old frontier stories, authentic or not. And Hart was growing old while still continuing to play the same parts. But more than that, he began to shift from his emphasis on honesty and

50

spend more time playing himself. Nowhere was this more evident than in his 1923 spectacular, *Wild Bill Hickok.*

If ever the dime novelists by their literary surgery had remade the image of the authentic gunfighter, they did it with James Butler Hickok. And Hickok, not being opposed to glamorous publicity, helped them by strutting around with starched collars, a Zouave jacket, a flashy red vest, and telling the tallest tales about his exploits. For example, his first killing occurred when he was in a concealed position and shot an unarmed man. "Wild Bill" told the jury that he fought his opponent in the classic toe-to-toe gun-fighting style. This murder was unusual for Hickok. Actually he was a very tough and brave fighter. He served heroically in the Civil War as a wagonmaster and scout, meeting and developing a close friendship with "Buffalo Bill" Cody. Later the two fought bravely together in the Indian campaigns, and Cody invited Hickok to join his Wild West show. (Hickok joined it briefly, but had to leave because everyone was getting sick of his mean practical jokes on the Indian actors and his frequent barroom brawls.) Following the Civil War, "Wild Bill" made his living as a gambler and a marshal. You could sum up his career in those days in four words: poker, booze, politics and prostitutes. Bill had his own way of enforcing the law; he'd set up his office in the back of a bordello and then put an end to anyone who interfered with the operation of his crimes. The local authorities didn't mind in those days. They had hired him for his guns, not for his morality. But that soon changed too, and Hickok drifted from town to town, winding up his days in Deadwood. He had come there with Calamity Jane to see if he could regain some of his lost money. It was during one of his continuous poker games that he was shot in the head by a frightened man who thought Bill was out to gun him down. At the time, Hickok was holding two aces and two eights, which became known in western folklore as "the deadman's hand."

Obviously there was plenty of material for William Hart to work with in his movie. Instead, he indulged himself in all his old clichés, and the audience saw the same old stuff all over again. What was particularly annoying was Hart's romanticizing of Hickok's shooting exploits. In one scene of the movie, "Wild Bill" places his shooting irons on the floor to show his enemies just how quick he really was. That stunt might be fine for other films, but coming from a star who prided himself on presenting the authentic West, it was terrible. Here was a cowboy who attacked others for their "glaring errors," but forgot that the first code of the gunfighter was self-preservation. The actual Hickok, by necessity not cowardice, never took chances. For example, during the eight months he was marshal of Abilene, "Wild Bill" carefully avoided any bright lights or murky alleyways. He made it a point of patrolling the streets in the center of the road while he sent his untrustworthy deputies on the walkways—just in case of surprise attacks. And anytime he faced a large crowd, in- or out-of-doors, Hickok kept his back to a wall. Did it seem likely then that such a gunman would put his pistols down before his enemies?

Situations like this plus the repetitious treatments of the West eventually got Hart in trouble with his producers. In 1925, he signed a contract with United Artists to release his last film *Tumbleweeds*. The agreement stated that the company would exert every effort to give the movie first-class treatment. But when it was released, *Tumbleweeds* appeared only in cheap theaters and received almost no advanced publicity. Hart was shocked, but no one in the industry seemed to care. He, for some unknown reason, was unwelcome in the movie world. Years after, he won a quarter-of-a-million dollar lawsuit from the company he could have been a partner in. But once more his court victory came too late. He was finished with movies.

He retired to his ranch, proud and undefeated. He refused to compromise his principles and make the kind of movies that others wanted from him. He looked back on what he had accomplished in the past decade. Almost singlehandedly, William Surrey Hart had taken the western movie from a dead end and given it the greatest stature any film type had ever received. He had made its cowboy heroes more popular and famous than any other created in the history of this country.

(*left*) A real life picture of John H. ("Doc") Holliday. From a photograph in *Human Life*, May, 1907.

(THE KANSAS STATE HISTORICAL SOCIETY, TOPEKA)

After Tombstone, Wyatt Earp came back to Dodge City to settle some of the town's troubles. At the "Dodge City Peace Commission" of 1883, William Barclay ("Bat") Masterson is second from the right in the back row, and Wyatt is second from the left in the front row.

(THE KANSAS STATE HISTORICAL SOCIETY, TOPEKA)

(*right*) The real Wyatt Earp. From a photograph in *Human Life,* May, 1907. (THE KANSAS STATE HISTORICAL SOCIETY, TOPEKA)

The Long Branch Saloon in Dodge City is the model for most of the famous barroom scenes in western films about whiskey, wild women and tinhorn gamblers. (THE KANSAS STATE HISTORICAL SOCIETY, TOPEKA)

This is the famous Front Street in Dodge City, Kansas, in 1878, where shootings, fights and killings reached an all-time high.

Wyatt Earp (Henry Fonda) makes it clear to "Doc" Holliday (Victor Mature) that the marshal is the law in Tombstone in this scene from John Ford's *My Darling Clementine* (1946).

Joel McCrea (Wyatt Earp) stands over his opponents in Jacques Tourneur's *Witchita* (1955). (ALLIED ARTISTS)

Henry Fonda, with a small group of men, attempts to stop a lynching in William Wellman's *The Ox-Bow Incident* (1943).

Frank (Henry Fonda) and Jesse (Tyrone Power) find that bank robbing is not as easy as holding up trains in Henry King's *Jesse James* (1939).

(*left*) Never was there more controversy over sex in the Western than when Rio (Jane Russell) became the girl friend of Billy the Kid (Jack Beutel) in Howard Hughes's *The Outlaw* (1943).

No heroes have ever proved more durable in the history of western folklore than the Lone Ranger and Tonto. Here are their two most famous actors—Jay Silverheels and Clayton Moore—in *The Lone Ranger and the Lost City of Gold* (1958).

YEARS OF GREED
AND GREATNESS

Those who made the cowboy films shared some of the values and misfortunes of the bold pioneers who had tamed the Far West more than fifty years before. They too gambled that the Pacific Coast offered tremendous opportunities for anyone who had the courage to try his luck. They considered no hardship too great, no risk too dangerous for a rugged and aggressive individualist. Like the original Eastern pioneers who came West, innocent of their undertaking, the ambitious tycoons distrusted the barons of big business, priding themselves instead on their economic self-sufficiency. And like many of the settlers who put their future in land development, the movie moguls following World War I bought large chunks of theatrical real estate at fantastic prices. Not having the needed funds, the film giants turned to the money men of Wall Street, dangerously overextending themselves by borrowing heavily and going into enormous debt. Few of them doubted the wisdom of such actions; they believed in their future and that of the industry itself. The most phenomenal

60

year of all was 1919. Famous Players—Lasky, for example, negotiated a ten-million-dollar loan to buy movie theaters galore. Louis B. Mayer, who in 1907 began building a film empire, spent a fortune for his own Los Angeles studio. (Incidentally, Mayer's early fortune was the result of his having the exclusive exhibition rights of *The Birth of a Nation* in New England.) Still in 1919, Marcus Loew borrowed over nine million dollars to purchase more cinema palaces, hereafter known as Loew's Incorporated. Within twelve months, following the example of his competitors, he took over the faltering Metro Company as protection against being overcharged for a regular supply of films. This meant acquiring another three-million-dollar loan. And still he wasn't satisfied. He now wanted to merge his production unit with that of Mayer's and with the Goldwyn Company, a firm started in 1916 after Sam Goldwyn abruptly exited from the newly formed Famous Players-Lasky operation and joined the Selwyn brothers. (Goldwyn himself was not involved in the new merger, having gone off in 1922 to make millions with his own production outfit.) Loew finally got his wish in 1924 when the complicated negotiations finalized into Metro-Goldwyn-Mayer, with Louis B. Mayer as production head. Within a year he suffered a heart attack, eventually dying in 1927. All this fantastic wheeling and dealing among the movie moguls was pushing many of them toward eventual disaster, but everything looked marvelous as the Twenties began. The stability of western movies at the box-office was partly responsible for this outlook.

No better illustration of the close relationship between the cowboy pictures and the film tycoons existed than in the situation of William Fox. Like most of his successful rivals at the top, he was a Jewish immigrant, reared in poverty with little formal education. His major ambition was to be the biggest and the best in the film world, and he lived accordingly. Legend has it the hardworking mogul never carried a watch and almost always had the windows of his office covered to hide the time of day. Fox believed that a man quit work when he finished what was on his desk. For someone who crowded a lot into a day, this often meant going without sleep for thirty-six hours. To his credit, he never hesitated to work as long as he had to, or harder than anyone he employed.

Like his contemporaries, he came to movies with little understanding of show business, and even less knowledge about film making. In 1904, one of his get-rich schemes had led him to a Brooklyn penny arcade at a moment in history when most people considered movies a passing fancy. But Fox was impressed by the large crowds that filed continually into the basement to watch the short one-reelers. Not until he had invested his life savings of sixteen hundred dollars did the twenty-five year old businessman realize that his quickly vanishing patrons had been hired by the previous owner to fool the prospective buyer. But Fox shrugged off the past and soon owned fifteen theaters, which he eventually turned into the highly successful General New York Film Rental Group. Encouraged by his impressive achievement, Fox fought the Trust because it stood in his way, at the same time starting his own production unit when the Patents people cut off his supply of films for exhibition.

When the Twenties began, Fox headed a vast empire worth millions of dollars. Like Zukor, Lasky, Goldwyn, Mayer and others, a major portion of his fortune was made by capitalizing on the star system and the production of western movies, regarded as sure money-makers at the box-office. Each studio had its own favorite personality who repeated his familiar role in film after film. Fox was more fortunate than most because he employed one of the greatest cowboy heroes of all time: Tom Mix.

Born in 1880, Mix appeared, at least according to press reports, the most authentic adventurer in silent film history. For the first thirty years of his life, this soldier of fortune had

62

fought in the Spanish American War in the Philippines, the Boxer Rebellion in China, and the Boer War in Africa. At other times he worked as a Texas Ranger, a sheriff, and a United States Deputy Marshal. Afterwards, Mix became a champion rodeo star with the Miller Brothers 101 Ranch. About 1910, this fabulous man decided to buy a large ranch of his own and take life a little easier.

When Selig made it known that same year that he needed a ranch for his western movies, Mix offered him not only his place but also his services. Before very long the rugged cowboy was writing, directing and performing in a host of commonplace one-, two- and three-reelers aimed at exploiting the nation's fascination with Westerns. But Selig pictures did nothing for their star. And so for seven undistinguished years Mix worked in the shadow of Broncho Billy and later William S. Hart. Then, in 1917, the thirty-seven year old cowboy caught the attention of Fox, and he switched studios.

Fox may not have known much about production, but he knew a lot about exhibition. And he knew that to try to compete with the great Hart by imitating his good-badman image would never be quite as successful as creating a new and unique screen sagebrush hero. Counseled by his employer, Mix developed a counter image to the Famous Players-Lasky star. While Hart depicted the westerner as a heavy drinker, humorless and lonely, Mix created the carefree cowboy who never smoked, drank or cursed. In fact, the only time he ever entered a saloon was to punish some villain. (Interestingly enough, Mix, in real life, had lavish bars installed in his cars.) The new hero, in somewhat of a return to the earlier and simpler Westerns, donned a big white hat and always defeated the obvious and completely evil opposition. Unlike Hart's characters, who had complex personalities and underwent transformations during the course of the movie, a Mix role was straightforward, presenting an individual who found himself caught up in someone else's difficulties, solved them,

63

and accepted or got little thanks for his efforts. Since Hart's films avoided stunt work and fancy tricks, the Fox star went out of his way to include spectacular riding sequences and superb rope-twirling episodes in his adventures, even when they added little to the story. He reasoned that his movies were made mostly for kids, and youngsters preferred lots of action to a logical tale. Then too, he felt his audiences were bored, as he was, with realistic films. They came to movies for escape and entertainment, not for accuracy.

Mix also added glamor to his off-screen life, which both Fox and he knew would appeal to his audiences and help the sale of his pictures. He wore ostentatious hand-tailored, white western outfits, magnificent boots, diamond-studded belts and pearl-inlaid pistols. He owned the fastest, most expensive and luxurious cars, some with large steer horns on the radiators. His mansion displayed on its roof an enormous electric sign which proclaimed the name of Tom Mix for all to see day and night. And in his dining room, there was a fountain that flowed in a variety of stunning colors. Only a respected and experienced adventurer like Mix could appear so much the dandy and still earn the awe of western fans. And only someone earning $17,000 a week could afford it!

When sound came into films near the end of the decade, the importance of cowboy stars including Mix, declined. Although Mix traveled from one studio to the next after 1927, he never made it back to the top. After 1935, his movie days ended, he kept in the public eye by touring in rodeo shows. Then on October 12, 1940, at sixty years of age, Tom Mix accidentally drove his speeding automobile off a highway and died instantly. Although he had never made one great movie, his actions and methods had firmly established a cowboy image that still exists today in many film and television Westerns.

Even in the Twenties, Mix, like Hart, had dozens of imitators. One of the better romantic copies was Hoot Gibson, the man with a boy's face and a clown's heart. Like Mix, he too had come from the Miller Brothers 101 Ranch and Selig pictures. And he had among his laurels the distinction of being 1912's World Championship Cowboy. Whereas Fox had helped to make Mix a star, Carl Laemmle, "the little giant" who had done more than anyone to bring the powerful Trust to its knees, started Gibson on his way to fame and fortune in 1916. "Uncle Carl," as he was affectionately known to employees, followed the pattern of the large exhibitors of the era and in 1912 had bought himself a production unit to insure a steady flow of films for his many movie houses, all at reasonable rentals. Soon IMP became Universal Pictures, and it needed its share of cowboy stars. Although World War I interrupted Gibson's career for two years, he was back at his job shooting and fighting with Western badmen by 1919. It was then that he began developing a series of slow-paced cowboy movies in which he continually appeared as an easygoing wrangler whose delightful sense of humor, carefully balanced with good riding and fast fists, made him one of the most beloved cowboy heroes of the Jazz Age.

Another Mix imitation was the spectacular, handsome, and witty Ken Maynard. Neither he nor Gibson ever attempted to make quality Westerns. Instead Ken preferred to play his part with showmanship and offer the audiences excitement and fast-paced adventure. Typical of the search for similar Mix stars, Maynard also had earned fame as a rodeo rider, having won the National Trick Riding Championship in 1920. By 1924 he was making cheaply-put-together films—or "B" pictures as they are known in film history—which supported the studio efforts of the larger and more expensive "A" pictures, as well as provided a training ground for new directors, technicians and performers.

There were other western stars as well, and every one of them made his annual share of cowboy pictures, close to a hundred such films each season. If you can picture seeing the same story a dozen different ways for more than a decade, then you will understand that not even the superb actions of a Hart or Mix would be enough to bolster an audience that was once more getting tired of cowboy movies. Box-office receipts again were dwindling for the western adventure, and producers began to fear that the popularity of the filmed frontier had finally ended. Then, once again in 1923, Famous Players-Lasky revolutionized western film history. Ironically, it was the same year that Pop Lubin, the man who had saved them almost a decade before, died, ignored by the industry he had a role in creating.

The major events, according to Lasky in his autobiography *I Blow My Own Horn,* began on one of his endless trips between the New York and Hollywood offices. As he was leaving to catch a train west, his secretary gave him a copy of Emerson Hough's *The Covered Wagon,* a best-selling novel about the Oregon Trail. He argued that he did not have time to read it, preferring instead to scan a synopsis of the plot. But the persistent employee claimed that no summary could be written that would do justice to the excitement of the book itself. So Lasky boarded the train, and as he sped past Kansas he began to read the account of the hardy pioneers of 1848–49 who had traveled across the plains and through the mountains. And as he read, he recalled how his grandfather had told him stories about the American dream, a land where a rugged individual with only his rifle, wagon and livestock could become the equal of any man.

By the time Lasky arrived at the Hollywood studio, he was determined to make the film on a grand style. And why not? In spite of what the audiences currently felt about western movies, what stories were better suited for *moving* pictures? The essence of film was motion, and every good producer and director knew that the secret of a successful film centered on movement. *The Covered Wagon* was perfect for the screen because everything could easily be translated into visual action: for example, the motion of the prairie schooners rolling

66

west against the horizon, the circular motion of the attacking Indians, and the excitement of the livestock moving across the great rivers. Much to the producer's horror, the film had already been assigned to a very efficient but hardly creative director. To compound his problems, the role of the sturdy heroine had been given to a delicate and sophisticated actress who specialized in society characterizations. The first order of business, therefore, required pulling the props out from under the current production plans. Lasky convinced the unsuspecting director that Westerns were only for new men at the studio who had to prove themselves, and romanced the star by explaining that she was meant for gowns, not gingham. Next Lasky considered the best person to take charge of the movie. He had heard rumors that James Cruze, a recently converted actor turned director, had Indian blood and was born in Nevada. Lasky felt this man was, without question, ideal for the assignment. Thus by chance, Cruze, who has often been referred to by film historians as an almost good director, entered the ranks of screen immortals.

Everyone at the West Coast studio soon became very excited about the film. Any regard for a tight budget disappeared. The starting figure was $500,000, or what today would be worth about seven million dollars. (By the time production finished, the movie cost another $250,000.) Soon after the new plans got underway, Lasky got a long distance phone call from Zukor. Calmly the man in New York inquired if there wasn't some mistake in the cost of this recent Western *The Covered Wagon*. "No," Lasky explained, "it was an E-P-I-C." For a moment there was silence in the East. And then in quiet tones, the amazing Zukor said, "An epic, eh? Well, that's different. You go ahead . . ."

After numerous locations were tested, Cruze finally decided to make his native Nevada the scene of the first western spectacular. To avoid any unnecessary interruptions, he selected the quarter-of-a-million-acre Baker Ranch in Snake Valley as the site to erect five hundred tents, a makeshift city to shelter nearly a thousand actors, technicians and extras collected for the movie.

Then for eight weeks Cruze recreated the story of the dauntless pioneers who blazed an incredible trail across the dangerous prairies, mountains and rivers that stood between them and the promised lands of Oregon and California. In ten reels of uneven quality, audiences witnessed and sometimes felt part of the struggles and the divisions of the romantic wagon train.

In the character of Jesse Wingate (Charles Ogle) we were able to sense something of the missionary zeal and farm lust of the men who traveled west at the average rate of three miles a day to find their homestead of milk and honey. Roles like that of Jim Bridger (Tully Marshall) and Jackson (Ernest Torrance) gave us insights into the nature of the pathfinders of another era; men more akin to a reckless savage life and eager to escape the unbearable restrictions of civilization. Unfortunately for the stars of the film, the script forced them into a ridiculous love triangle from the start of the picture to the end, and the less said about their performances and parts, the more charitable.

But Karl Brown's inspired camera work more than made up for the inept script, beginning with the wagon train leaving Westport Landing (now Kansas City). He showed us visually a composite jumping-off place of all the last outposts of law and order where the value of money ended and the test of a person's endurance began. Time and time again the audience witnessed such magnificent shots as the lonely prairie schooners etched against the landscape as they rolled in single file under an awesome sky, the frightening attack of wild Indians, a stunning fire on the plains, the thrills of a buffalo hunt and the exciting fording of a swollen river. The pseudo-documentary approach of the film added a certain sense of reality to the situations.

68

Without a doubt, Cruze's significant achievement lay in his visual treatment of courageous families who tested their strength against the unknown. But he was wrong when he claimed, "There wasn't a false whisker in the film." Although the studio had hired the respected Tim McCoy, a professional soldier and acknowledged Indian authority, there was not much authenticity in the film. (Shortly after, McCoy began his own western roles which were extremely popular at M-G-M.) The pseudo-documentary style of the picture masked for many viewers, but not for film historians, the incredible attitudes of the pioneers who remained seemingly unconcerned by the journey which took them along the same route as the Donner Party, where the forty-five starving survivors had to eat the bodies of thirty-six dead companions, where the climate threatened to snuff out their lives, and where incensed Indians tried desperately to stop the flood of intruders into their country. One also had reason to doubt McCoy's scholarship concerning the Indians when he stood by while they were characterized as ignorant and savage warriors. (Few believed that Cruze had any Red blood in him after the way he presented his supposed relatives.) No less than the studio's famous star, William S. Hart, questioned the reality of the situations presented, calling particular attention to the stupidity of a wagonmaster who would settle his followers in a boxed canyon at the mercy of an unseen enemy, or the absurdity of having cattle fording a river with heavy neck yokes, worn in the real West only for strenuous wagon work.

Yet for 1923, *The Covered Wagon* demonstrated a marvelous grandeur as well as the beginning of the epic western tradition, and the film broke existing attendance records wherever it played. No one directly in charge of the production—Zukor, Lasky, or Cruze—seemed to really understand why. When the two production heads saw the original print, they both felt something was lacking. Lasky suggested they insert a scene showing the hardy pioneers reaching Oregon, one of their party scooping up a shovel of rich soil, and everyone dropping to his knees giving thanks to his Savior. While Jesse made the scene, Adolph tested the two versions: one without prayer, one with. Naturally, they preferred the religious version. Cruze himself thought that his long shots of the action were the best way to create the excitement of the perilous journey, rarely applying the excellent editing ideas Griffith had established the previous ten years for intercutting various types of shots into spectacular scenes. For the moment, it didn't matter as long as the picture was a hit.

In that same year, the brilliant cowboy comedian, Will Rogers, made a parody of the movie entitled *Two Wagons— Both Covered,* showing that the treacherous trip ended with the exhausted pioneers having to buy their land from dishonest real estate agents. But as always in a Rogers' comedy, there was an element of truth. Many of the actual farmers who had gone west before the Civil War, found themselves ruined after 1870 by their inability to stand up against the land speculators and the advancing city slickers. Perhaps the well-known American poet Edwin Markham, son of pioneer parents from Oregon and California, described the situation best in his outraged poem of 1899, "The Man With the Hoe." He wrote that the once mighty and independent yeoman had become a symbol of ". . . humanity betrayed, plundered, profaned and disinherited. . . ."

Just once more during the silent days of film, Cruze approached greatness in 1925 when he attempted to recreate the visual record of the riders of the pony express, with an emphasis on Indians, road agents and romance. Apart from the director's usual difficulties in balancing history and fiction, *The Pony Express* had some very charming western touches. One of the most memorable included George Bancroft as the villain Jack Slade, who is trying to convince Ricardo Cortez as Jack Weston, the hero, that the heroine is his girl. Suddenly Slade draws his gun and shoots clean through a bottle being carried by an innocent bypasser across the street. Just as suddenly, Weston whips out his weapon and places a bullet through the neck of the same bottle, still held by the terrified stranger. The two antagonists understood each other.

But, as before, praise was reserved for the film's visual splendor. In seeing it again and again, one comes away with a growing appreciation for the way Cruze captures the image of the mail-riders starting out from St. Joseph, Missouri, on their way to Sacramento, California, racing their horses across the country, stopping only for a change of mounts, and then onward through the dry, dusty valleys, up and over the snow-covered Sierras.

An interesting sidelight to *The Pony Express* was that, at the end, the villain escaped unpunished for his many crimes. What made this so unusual was that three years before, under pressure from their Wall Street investors, the film tycoons had asked Will Hays, the ex-Postmaster General of the United States, to head an office to clean up the scandal-ridden industry and the over-emphasis in American films on liquor, lewd women and luxurious living. Consequently, the conservative movie czar began insisting that anyone who committed a crime in a motion picture had to be punished by the last reel. Nevertheless, Cruze insisted on historical accuracy for his treatment of the real and notorious Jack Slade. The actual bad-man who had lived during the early days of the mail-riders in Julesburg, Colorado (the setting of the film), was a terror when drunk, and had actually done a number of things alluded to in the movie. But Slade finally left Julesburg and made his way to wild Virginia City in Montana, where the citizens had the local vigilantes hang him in the streets on March 10, 1864. Interestingly enough, when the studio remade the film in 1953, the opportunistic badman was gone along with the role of Jack Weston. Now Buffalo Bill (Charlton Heston) and Wild Bill Hickok (Forrest Tucker) shared the responsibility for getting the mail through in ten days, less

71

than half the time it took the Overland Stage Company. Five months later, that same year, United Artists released a sympathetic biographical movie of the notorious killer entitled *Jack Slade*, in which Mark Stevens starred and co-directed. Although the film tried to capitalize on the gunman's contributions to the growth of the Overland Trail and his friendship with Mark Twain, it was a monotonous and uninteresting account of a man who spent too much time in saloons.

As for the western film in the last few years of the Twenties, it too appeared repetitious and dull. Nevertheless, one man, more than any other in the decade, tied together the traditions and techniques of the past twenty years and began a new cycle of films of the frontier. His name is John Ford, the most prominent and successful director of cowboy pictures in film history.

❧ Christened Sean O'Fearna in Cape Elizabeth, Maine, on February 1, 1895, John Ford has been making movies for over fifty-six years. Besides the distinction as being the only Hollywood director to win six Academy Awards—also four New York Film Critics' Awards—he maintains the rank of retired Rear Admiral in the United States Navy.

❧ At nineteen, Ford, lured away from the University of Maine by his popular serial star-brother Francis, began work for Universal Studios as a property man, assistant director, and stuntman. It was not uncommon in those early years to find the ambitious youngster dressed as a cavalry trooper disciplining troublesome Indians in the morning, and after a lunch break, joining in as one of the breakaway Redmen. By the time he was twenty-one, Ford had caught the attention of Carl Laemmle and was given a chance to direct his own films, many of which starred Harry Carey and Hoot Gibson.

❧Although the three men got along extremely well and remained lifelong friends, Ford appears to have had the greatest influence on Carey. The cowboy actor, who had come to Universal in 1912 after a career on the stage and a series of films with the Biograph Studios under Griffith, imitated the cowpunchers created by Hart. This image persisted as he teamed up with Ford to write and star in their type of good-badman film; mostly character stories featuring lots of hard-riding, two-fisted action and plenty of excitement. The actor's familiar costume, according to Ford himself, was created by the two of them as a reaction against the fancy-dressed sage-brush heroes of the time. Carey made it a point of wearing worn-out clothes with patches and almost never carried a gun. (Gibson, too, refused to carry a weapon, borrowing one from a friend when the last action scene required a gunfight.) In many respects, the Ford-Gibson-Carey films provided the training grounds for the director's later motion pictures, especially in his depiction of the rugged heroes who often sat around poetic campfires and populated frontiers where rough humor and friendship gave an added dimension to the epic stories of Ford's romantic and nostalgic West.

In 1922, William Fox offered Ford a job and within a year, John, as he now called himself, began directing on a full-time basis. For the most part, the freedom he had enjoyed so much at Laemmle's studio was gone, most of his working time now being given to assigned films carefully controlled by the front office. But once in a while Ford was given the opportunity to make his brand of Western. His first opportunity, his third film for Fox, came in 1924, when the studio decided to cash in on the popularity of *The Covered Wagon*.

The Iron Horse dramatized the remarkable courage, strength and energy of Irish and Chinese laborers who joined a continent together with steel and blood. Ford, like Cruze, faced major script difficulties which seriously weakened the effectiveness of the actual motion picture. The poorly written screenplay centered its attention on a brave son's revenge for his father's murder, but more often than not Ford managed to set his camera's eye on the stirring construction of the first transcontinental railroad.

In almost every respect, Ford's work overshadowed Cruze's efforts. Not only did the final film run twelve reels, two more than *The Covered Wagon*, but the behind-the-scenes preparations staggered the film world's imagination. Although Nevada was again the location, the studio built two complete towns instead of a tent city, hired five thousand people to recreate the epic achievement, and used more than twenty-five thousand cattle, horses and buffalo to depict the actual events.

Even more impressive, Ford's skill in presenting historical events clearly elevated him above the work of men like Cruze and Hart. The former specialized in semi-documentary snatches of the past, caught in long shots, held for a moment and then passed over. Hart preferred dusty, somber episodes of tough men playing their parts against a neutral background. Ford, however, lovingly romanticized the heroic qualities of sturdy heroes pitted against magnificent landscapes and staged history for his personal satisfaction. Having once worked with Griffith (he reportedly had been a clansman in *The Birth of a Nation*) and obviously influenced by the brilliant director, Ford knew how to build, compose and manipulate action scenes in such a way that each member of the audience became a part of the struggle. Unfortunately, then and now, he is an impatient man who dislikes redoing a scene. His preference for spontaneity, more than perfection, mars a few episodes in a majority of his pictures.

Nevertheless, his insistence on naturalness usually results in strong performances by his casts. Certainly his handling of George O'Brien turned the bit player into a star. The former light heavyweight boxing champion of the Pacific Fleet in World War I, stunt man, part-time cameraman for several Mix films had been around for a few years and had gotten no place in movies. But working for half a year with John Ford made him a much sought after performer.

The director's next and last important silent Western came in 1926, *Three Bad Men*. This time the main characters were a trio of outlaws who sought to prove to themselves and to a woman that they were both honorable and brave. Ford made greater use of the physical environment in this movie than he had ever done before, and many of the scenes in the dance hall, the shambles of the old church and the Mojave Desert tested the heroes' quest for respect.

Three Bad Men also introduced many of the great director's trademarks. Whereas Sergeant Slattery of *The Iron Horse* established Ford's fondness for the rowdy and endearing professional Irishman, the new film produced the fashionable sheriff, the outspoken and drunken journalist, and the reformed badmen who in the end give up their lives for others. Then, too, there were the unforgettable black and white portraits of men on horseback in the distant sunset, and the Indians lurking on the crest of some menacing hill.

Otherwise it was all over for the silent days of western movies. The coming of sound, coupled with the crippling Depression of 1929, began to destroy many of those who thought themselves indestructible.

Gregory Peck plays one of two brothers, both in love with the desirable and dangerous half-breed Indian girl (Jennifer Jones), in Henry King's *Duel in the Sun* (1946). (SELZNICK)

(*right*) Lance Pool (Robert Taylor) and Orrie Masters (Paula Raymond) discuss the white man's prejudice against Indians in Anthony Mann's *Devils Doorway* (1950). (BETTMANN/SPRINGER FILM ARCHIVE)

Tom Jeffords (James Stewart) and his bride Sonseeahray (Debra Paget) agree with Cochise (Jeff Chandler) that peace must come in spite of the white man's deception in Delman Daves' *Broken Arrow* (1950).

John Ford recreates a version of Custer's last stand in his cavalry film *Fort Apache* (1948). Left to right (*center*): Henry Fonda, Dick Foran, John Wayne (kneeling), Ward Bond and Victor McLaglen.

Gregory Peck as Johnny Ringo, the pathetic gunslinger who tries to escape from his reputation in Henry King's *The Gunfighter* (1950).

(BETTMANN/SPRINGER FILM ARCHIVE)

(*left*) Wayne losing control of the cattle drive in Howard Hawks's *Red River* (1948). Montgomery Clift, with a butt in his mouth, prepares to intervene.   (UNITED ARTISTS)

The second of Ford's romantic cavalry trilogy about a tough commander who has one last misson against rebellious Indians before he retires in *She Wore A Yellow Ribbon* (1949). Ben Johnson stands by John Wayne as both pay their respect to a loved one's memory. (RKO-RADIO)

Jack Palance as a murderous Indian who goes on a rampage against the
white man in Charles Warren's *Arrowhead* (1953).   (PARAMOUNT)

(*left*) James Stewart (Lin McAdam) gets tough with Dan Duryea (Waco
Johnnie Dean) in Anthony Mann's *Winchester '73* (1950).

(BETTMANN/SPRINGER FILM ARCHIVE)

The last of Ford's great trilogy about the soldiers of the Old West was this tale of a hardened cavalry commander (John Wayne) who leads his troops against a band of savage Indians in *Rio Grande* (1950).　　(REPUBLIC)

OUT OF POVERTY ROW

During 1926, box-office receipts around the country began taking a serious nose dive, and the film tycoons sensed they had another business crisis on their hands. The reasons for the sharp reversals soon became clear: too many new film palaces being built too quickly and too closely together; too many extravagant and repetitious movies failing with an increasingly discriminating audience, and far too much charged for tickets when fans could just as well get their entertainment from an inexpensive new toy at home—the "radio." Something had to be done to get back the regular film customers. A novelty would do it.

The novelty was sound pictures, "talkies." The idea had been around since the beginning of motion pictures, and several corporations were in the process of refining their experiments. William Fox, in fact, was trying his Movietone methods out in several theaters. But the glory went to the four sons of an immigrant Polish cobbler.

More than twenty years before, the Warner brothers— Harry, Sam, Albert and Jack—gladly rejected their unromantic lives as butchers, salesmen and shopowners and turned instead to the exciting field of moving pictures. Their progress had been along the by-now familiar route of the film tycoons—from exhibitors to distributors and eventually, in 1919, to successful producers. When borrowing large sums of money became fashionable, they followed the trend and quickly overextended themselves. Yet for a while it looked as if they would be able to make the grade. But when business went bad for the industry, it was especially hard on them.

Film historians record that the Western Electric-Electrical Research Bell Telephone Laboratories at first took their new sound device known as "Vitagraph" to such fabulous showmen as Zukor and Laemmle, the once bold and daring young men who less than a decade before had toppled the mighty film Trust. But success had dimmed their courage, and caution suggested that they refuse the new invention. So it was that Vitagraph came to the Warner brothers, who agreed to gamble their future on its success . . . and won. Near the end of 1927, Al Jolson, starring in the Warner Brothers' production *The Jazz Singer*, proved that caution and conservatism in the movie industry are the surest ways to obscurity. Audiences returned by the millions to see and hear the talkies.

Not everyone was thrilled by the turn of events. The sensational appeal of sound movies created tremendous problems for the studios and terrible hardships for their employees, including thousands of cowboy stars, extras, and stuntmen. Producing talkies meant changing equipment and techniques as well as finding suitable performers who could *speak* and act. Everything was in a state of turmoil, and until the monarchs of the studios knew which way to go they issued orders to slow down on the number of pictures being made, hold off on hiring any new stars, and reconsider renewing old contracts, particularly those belonging to the highly-paid stars of the now dead silent era. In addition, hastily constructed soundproof-studios were built, and the once popular, noisy outdoor locations and stories either got curtailed or eliminated

84

from the current production plans. Imagine the effect on all those people who had migrated west in the previous twenty years to act in the hundreds of successful cowboy films. Many had no choice but to go back where they came from. Westerns were out.

Besides cheering the novelty of talking, singing and dancing movies, the public made it clear that the theaters needed improving and the sound techniques needed refinement. So once more the ambitious movie moguls, in need of vast sums of money, trudged into the offices of the conservative and cautious industrialists. Although the money was available and the film companies could get onto the stock market, certain conditions had to be agreed to. Changes had to be made in management, in operational procedures and in the types of pictures made on the West Coast. As for Westerns, their production was more sharply reduced than at present, owing to their apparent unpopularity at box-offices everywhere. No one wanted to invest millions of dollars in worn-out formulas. Boston banker Joseph Kennedy typified the situation. The father of the thirty-fifth President of the United States owned, in the late 1920's, a large chain of theaters—Keith, Albee, Orpheum—and had increased his holdings by merging his interests with the Film Booking Office of America. Now with the patents for sound pictures locked in the hands of a relatively few companies, he decided to tie in with one of them, the Radio Corporation of America. The banner for the new merger read RKO-Radio Pictures. One of their first orders of business rid them of any commitments to western movies, a decision which removed Tom Mix from Hollywood for a few years. Except for Universal, the important studios followed the example of the times and stopped production of Westerns. Those cowboys who wanted to ride and shoot in pictures turned their hopes to the producers of "Poverty Row."

In Hollywood, in the last part of the Twenties, there existed near Gower Street a colony of minor movie producing companies including such firms as Invincible, Victory, Tiffany,

Monogram, and Mascot. These firms were known in the industry as "the producers of Poverty Row," because they were always short of funds, controlled no large chain of theaters which offered a ready outlet for their products, and had to distribute their pictures through the old, ineffective system of State's Rights Distribution. In spite of all this, many of the screen's most enduring stars emerged from their lots, or else came there to work between their "A" pictures for some extra money and good comradeship.

One of the most famous stories about Poverty Row concerns a dropout named Frank. Legend has it that he quit Grinnell College after his freshman year and met some friends while visiting Hollywood in December of 1924. They impressed the lanky six-footer with their stories of how falling off horses earned them ten dollars per day. The boys invited Frank to come with them to "Gower Gulch," as it was sometimes called, and hang around the stables. Usually when a studio hired a horse, it hired a couple of cowboys as well. The big fellow decided to try his luck, met several of the producers who took a liking to him, and for the next year-and-a-half worked regularly, taking more than his share of spills as an extra and stuntman. But once he saw Mix in operation and found out his salary, Frank was determined he could do as well. So he hired an agent. Her advice was to get a different name. Since there was already one Frank Cooper in the casting office, it was decided that he would be known as Gary Cooper. She also suggested that if the big studios wouldn't give him a screen test, he could make one himself.

Cooper did just that. For twenty-five dollars, he rented a horse, an empty lot and a fancy cowboy outfit. For forty dollars more, a cameraman agreed to shoot the test film. At the appropriate time, Gary Cooper galloped toward the camera, suddenly pulled back at the horse's reins causing the animal to rear up. Then when the horse came back down, Cooper leaped off the mount, hopped over a fence, whipped off his hat and bowed low to his imaginary audience. All this in forty seconds and one single take. But it got him a job at Paramount.

As Gary Cooper worked over the next three years to improve his status and his talents, so did the creative technicians of the important studios. Among their many advancements, they devised soundproof covers—*blimps*—to mask the sounds of the noisy camera enclosures, and they constructed special miscrophones designed to record only the sounds their heads pointed at. Later on these *directional* mikes hung from booms, which followed performers around. In addition, the studios, always fascinated with color and screen sizes, continued experimenting.

/ Near the end of the decade, an extraordinary performance by a former silent film actor as the dashing Cisco Kid gave new hope to western fans and actors alike. Based upon a popular O'Henry short story, Fox's *In Old Arizona*, directed by Raoul Walsh, portrayed the fearless antics of a happy-go-lucky bandit-hero who spoke witty dialogue in broken English, confused his enemies, loved beautiful women, and robbed from the rich to give to the poor. O'Henry had described his modern Robin Hood as a man of twenty-five who looked twenty, and probably had a lifespan up to twenty-six. For Warner Baxter it was the break of a lifetime. According to legend, director Walsh intended to play the role of the bandit himself, but an unlucky eye injury forced him to cancel his plans, and he turned the part over to the suave, handsome and dashing Baxter. So convincing was the actor's performance and speech that at the second annual meeting of the Motion Picture Academy, the members presented Baxter with the 1928/29 gold statuette (it wasn't called an "Oscar" until 1931) as the outstanding male performer of the year. Although he never again reached such heights, the impressive actor performed in movies until 1950, achieving a rise in popularity during the Forties in a series of films playing the role of a crime doctor, a physician who uses his medical skill to catch criminals.

↗ Walsh's direction of the great outdoor scenes and Baxter's popularity in the role of a once-popular silent film cowboy hero convinced the major studios that the time was right to begin a new series of historical western spectaculars. The cycle only lasted four years, but it created the basic principles for the next thirty years.

The first important step was made by Paramount. They put their money on an old favorite, *The Virginian.* (It had been remade once in 1923, Joel McCrea would make another in 1946, and sixteen years later the story would form the basis for a very successful 90-minute weekly television series.) This time, however, the starring role went to the studio's up-and-coming performer Gary Cooper, and overnight he became one of the country's most popular actors. Everywhere people exclaimed that he was the perfect western hero, and no scene in motion picture history has been more unconsciously referred to than the famous saloon meeting where Trampas (played magnificently by Walter Huston) arrogantly calls the Virginian a foul name. Suddenly the lanky, silent cowpuncher pulls out his gun, places it in Trampas's stomach, looks into his eyes, and gently replies, "If you want to call me that, smile!"

Director George Hill, almost forty years later, would repeat the romantic mood of that saloon encounter in the opening scene of his film *Butch Cassidy and the Sundance Kid.*

↖ Fox was not to be overshadowed by Zukor. He had developed not only an effective sound system but also a new screen size which he modestly called Grandeur. Once more he assigned Walsh to a Western, *The Big Trail,* giving him in addition to the new processes, a relatively free hand in the filming. The attempt in 1930 to capitalize on the familiar

88

ingredients of the past was obvious as once more audiences saw the frontiersmen gathering their wagons by the banks of the mighty Missouri, then heading westward to face painful and unexpected hardships. Once more a western director was hampered by a second-rate script, this one dealing with a hero intent on avenging his brother's murder. Only now the larger screen and the refined sound system added additional excitement to the buffalo stampede, the screaming Indian attack, and the fording of a swollen river. Fox premiered the spectacular at his newly acquired film palace, the Roxy, but his joy was short-lived. No one seemed to be particularly impressed by the movie.

Probably just as disappointed was the film's leading man who was making his screen debut as Breck Coleman, the trapper who scouted for the wagon train. Marian Michael Morrison, born May 26, 1907, had migrated to California from Iowa and had become one of the state's greatest football stars both at Glendale High School and the University of Southern California. During his summer vacations, he did odd jobs at the Fox studios and developed a lasting friendship with such people as John Ford and Raoul Walsh. When the latter looked about for a star lead in *The Big Trail*, he decided to give the young man a chance. But John Wayne, as he now called himself, had to wait nine more years until John Ford was ready to take a hand in his future.

A week before *The Big Trail* came to Broadway, M-G-M released its new Western, together with a sample of its experimental screen improvement called Realife. Although it had an advantage over Fox Grandeur, presenting a larger and wider picture, the images were not as sharp as those projected by Fox's method. Nevertheless, the new M-G-M film was far more popular.

In fact, director King Vidor's *Billy the Kid* became one of the most significant movies in the history of motion pictures for a very special reason; it was the model for hundreds of films dealing with range wars, corrupt sheriffs, and feuds between cattlemen and townspeople on the lawless frontier. It has also provided the screen and television with a fascinating character who has been portrayed by such popular performers as Roy Rogers, Robert Taylor, Audie Murphy, Scott Brady, Marlon Brando and Paul Newman. It seems worthwhile, therefore, to consider the facts about the actual Mr. Bonney, before we encounter the legendary Billy the Kid.

William Bonney was born in the New York City slums on November 23, 1859. By the time he was three, the family had moved west to Coffeyville, Kansas. After his father's death the boy and his mother left for Colorado, where she met and married William Antrim. Billy's stepfather then moved the family to Silver City, New Mexico, where the man worked in the mines, the mother ran a boardinghouse, and the boy ran wild.

Before his fifteenth birthday, William's mother died, and he took to a life of gambling, drinking and thievery. Many claims have been made that he was a killer by twelve years of age, but there is no evidence to support those stories. He was, however, a known thief and murderer by the fall of 1877, when he became a fugitive and fled to Lincoln County, New Mexico.

Lincoln County by then consisted of close to thirty thousand square miles of the richest grazing land known to cattlemen. It had been the reason that John S. Chisum had left Texas and driven his mighty cattle herds across the Rio Grande and established himself as the "King of the Pecos." Not only were there the great cattle trails, but also the booming cattle towns. And it was here that the greatest range war in the history of the American West would be fought.

Billy rode into the midst of a dangerous rivalry in the winter of 1877. Two vicious and violent gangs of outsiders had come to the territory to gain control of the rich banking and

90

10-26-1881
11-14-1881
1881
0-3-12

Full refund issued for new and unread books and unopened music within 30 days with a receipt from any Barnes & Noble store.

Store Credit issued for new and unread books and unopened music after 30 days or without a sales receipt. Credit issued at lowest sale price.

We gladly accept returns of new and unread books and unopened music from bn.com with a bn.com receipt for store credit at the bn.com price.

mercantile opportunities. On one side stood the "Santa Fe Ring," consisting of Lawrence Murphy, James Dolan, and John Riley. They were Easterners, and their greatest strength lay in their ability to manipulate the law to serve their interests. Consequently, Murphy's gang had its headquarters in Lincoln where they owned most of the stores, ran the powerful bank, and appointed their own lawman, Sheriff William Brady. On the other side stood the combine of John Tunstall and Alexander McSween, quietly supported by Chisum. Tunstall, an Englishman, had come to Lincoln county with the idea of making big money. He owned a large ranch and operated a big store in town. His affairs were handled mostly by McSween, an Eastern lawyer, who had first worked for the Santa Fe Ring, but thought his chances better with Tunstall so he left to join the Englishman in a profitable partnership. Basically, there was not much difference between the two gangs. Both wanted power and didn't quibble about how they obtained it.

Bonney began working for Murphy, but soon became attracted to Tunstall's mannerisms . . . and generous wages. He switched sides, and rumor has it the two became like "father and son."

Trouble began heating up when Tunstall found himself being undersold by Murphy men in cattle deals with the Army. To make matters worse, it became apparent that Murphy paid his men five dollars a head to rustle cattle from the opposition. Naturally, Sheriff Brady did nothing to interfere. Tunstall, in a fit of anger, dispatched a stinging letter to the Lincoln paper, denouncing Brady's corruption. The Sante Fe Ring retaliated quickly. They framed Tunstall on a cattle rustling charge and sent a posse led by deputy sheriffs Billy Morton and Frank Baker to bring in the "rustler." On February 18, 1878, John's four companions (including Billy) fled at the first sight of the posse, but the Englishman foolishly stayed to reason with the approaching men. Later it was reported that he was killed "resisting arrest." And thus began the Lincoln County wars.

McSween and Dick Brewer, Tunstall's foreman, quickly hired some gunslingers for revenge and protection. The foreman, through some questionable means, obtained a warrant for the arrest of the murderous posse, and went after them, capturing Morton and Baker. They were brought in dead, shot "trying to escape." But Murphy proved too powerful when it came to legal steps. He convinced the weak and ineffectual Governor Samuel B. Axtell to revoke Brewer's warrant and protect the Santa Fe Ring. He also had his men kill Brewer. On April 1st, Brewer's friends, in broad daylight and in the streets of Lincoln, ambushed and murdered Sheriff Brady and several of his deputies. (Billy the Kid always took part in the McSween gang fights, but there is no evidence that he directly shot any of Tunstall's killers.) Following the Brady shooting, the McSween gang hid in the hills, engaging in guerrilla activities for the next three months. But the feelings were building for a final showdown.

Then at high noon on Monday, July 15, 1878, the McSween gang rode into Lincoln determined to wipe out the Murphy-Dolan forces. But they failed and fled for cover in McSween's fortress-like house in town, where they were soon surrounded by Dolan's men, setting up their headquarters in Murphy's store. Shortly thereafter, a band of Mexicans rode into battle to support the McSween forces, but it was to no avail. A detachment of soldiers commanded by Lt. Col. Nathan Dudley entered the action, under the pretense of protecting the civilian population, but apparently to help the Dolan gang. The soldiers dispersed the Mexicans and mingled freely with McSween's enemies. (Later, Dudley was court-martialed but cleared of any misconduct.) The battle lasted for five days. Finally, on the 19th, someone gave the order to burn McSween out. The fire resulted in McSween's death and many of

92

his followers. History records that only four escaped, one of them was Billy the Kid. The Lincoln County War came to an end that afternoon, but not the career of Mr. Bonney.

He continued to steal and kill, eventually riding over to nearby Fort Sumner where he developed a drinking friendship with a bartender by the name of Patrick Floyd Garrett. They became known as "Little Casino" and "Big Casino," Garrett being over six feet tall. Then they parted ways, and Garrett was elected Sheriff of Lincoln in 1880. By this time President Rutherford Hayes, having gotten some idea of the trouble, removed Governor Axtell and appointed General Lew Wallace (the author of *Ben Hur*) in his place. Wallace met secretly with the Kid, but only broken promises resulted. Finally, the order went out to bring in Billy Bonney. Garrett captured the Kid, brought him back to a rigged trial where all of the Kid's enemies corrupted the court proceedings, and Billy returned to Lincoln to await his hanging on May 13, 1881. But the wild gunman made a daring escape, shooting down his two guards in cold blood. Garrett was extremely embarrassed by the event and promised to recapture Bonney.

Late on the night of July 14, the sheriff rode up to Pete Maxwell's house, hoping to find some information about Billy. He waited in a darkened room for someone to appear . . . alone and frightened. Then he heard a noise and saw a half-naked man, unarmed, approaching him asking "Who's there?" Without checking, Garrett quickly fired two shots at the figure, the second bullet going wild; and only afterwards did he realize that he had killed Billy the Kid. A year later Garrett co-authored a book claiming that he shot Bonney in a fair fight, but it just wasn't true. Twenty-seven years after Billy's death, Garrett, himself unarmed, was shot down by an angry rival rancher.

Following Billy's demise, dozens of books, magazines and newspaper articles appeared, depicting the psychopathic killer as either a Robin Hood or a devil. There was even a popular play in 1903. But then the interest died out, at least until 1926, when a Chicago reporter, Walter Noble Burns, published his romantic and totally unreliable book, *Saga of Billy the Kid*. In the Burns' version, Bonney, Tunstall and McSween were brave men who had been given a bad time by the sinister forces of Murphy, Dolan and Brady. Despite the falseness of the material and because of the renewed interest by the public in the accounts, M-G-M decided to make a movie of the events, and in 1930 one of the most significant Westerns ever made came to the screen.

Here was the basis for many of the Kid films to come; a lonely, handsome and confused young man in search of peace who runs into difficulty with a crooked sheriff. A feud erupts, and finally the Kid demands revenge, regardless of the consequences. All in all, about thirty people bite the dust before the film is over.

During this period in film history, Hollywood was quite concerned about its European film market. Consequently, it often made two versions of its better films, one for the home crowd and one for the foreign fans. For *Billy the Kid* M-G-M decided to have the Americans see an ending where Garrett allows Billy to ride off toward a Mexican retreat with his beautiful sweetheart. But overseas, the movie finished with a kindly Pat Garrett having to shoot Billy and then hold the dying Kid in his arms.

For the most part, director Vidor's work stands as one of the best visual representations of a lonely, violent society where strong and rugged men made their own laws and decided their own fate. Not only was the theme aided considerably by the harsh and realistic settings but also by the performances of the film's two leading players. Johnny Mack Brown, former All-American football star at the University of Alabama, never again demonstrated such acting talent as he did portraying the disturbed, sadistic and misunderstood outlaw hero. After this movie, he eventually decided to stay with cowboy roles and became one of the Western's most popular stars. Then, too, Wallace Beery, veteran actor of the silent days, also gave one of his finest performances as the friendly Pat Garrett.

But the most popular and spectacular Western yet made came from RKO-Radio, director Wesley Ruggles' *Cimarron*, released in January 1931. Based upon Edna Ferber's best-selling novel, the movie followed Yancey and Sabra Cravat through more than forty years of their turbulent lives. It shows how they raced to Oklahoma with thousands of other home-steaders in the great land rush of 1890, searching for the government's promised free land, staking their claim, only to lose it later. Eventually Yancey becomes a powerful force in the state, aided by the strength and intelligence of his wife. Richard Dix, already a big drawing card since his role as a mistreated Indian in *The Vanishing American* in 1925, gave the greatest performance of his career as the idealized, wan-dering adventurer. And for really the first time in western film history, the studios gave a female a place along with the men. Irene Dunne masterfully played the role of a resourceful and brave lady who took to the land and helped make it grow. Although both performers were nominated for Academy Awards in 1931, only the film won as best picture of the year, the only time a frontier story has ever been so honored.

Most people remember *Cimarron* as the last great Western of this short-lived period, but there was one more in February of 1932: Universal's *Law and Order*, directed by Edward Cahn. Not only did it have the flavor of the authentic West, but its story also provided the framework for yet another historical favorite of movie-goers. The screen credits gave William R. Burnett's novel *Saint Johnson* as the source of the plot, and the main characters were called Frame Johnson of Wichita (Walter Huston) and Ed Brandt (Harry Carey), but clearly the scriptwriter (John Huston) told the story of Wyatt Earp and Doc Holiday. The tales of these two men, like the Garrett-Bonney legends, became popular subjects for many films, including *My Darling Clementine* (1946),

Wichita (1955), and *Gunfight at the OK Corral* (1957). It also influenced the popular television series *Wyatt Earp*, which began its long reign in September 1956. Because of the many legends that have grown up around the notorious duo, we'd better examine the actual events that took place in Tombstone, Arizona, in 1881.

The main figure in the historical drama was Wyatt Earp, who in six short years, 1873–79 had gained a fabulous reputation as a tough lawman who helped tame Wichita and Dodge City. He had also won considerable notoriety as a tricky businessman, crooked gambler and unprincipled opportunist. Now, in December 1879, having heard about the trouble in the boomtown of Tombstone, actually the last of the violent towns in the aging wild frontier, the forty-one year old Earp came to seek new fortunes and fame. He brought with him his second wife (whom he later deserted, after which she turned to prostitution and suicide) and his brothers—Jim, Virgil and Morgan.

Accompanying the Earps was John H. Holliday, a tiny and sickly man who had started his murderous career by killing two "nigras" who wanted to share his swimming hole. Although he had graduated from college as a dentist, "Doc" preferred to make his way in the world with cards, guns and girls. Wyatt had first met Holliday in Dodge where the two men developed a lasting friendship, with Doc worshipping the lanky, pistol-whipping Earp.

Earp, proud, ambitious and dangerous, soon antagonized Sheriff Johnny Behan, a small and politically-motivated individual. Before long, Tombstone's most important citizens—saloon owners, gamblers, red-light girls and riffraff—were torn between the growing feud which simmered for more than a year. The turning point came in March 1881, when a Wells Fargo stage was held up and two posses rode out after the bandits, Sheriff Behan's and Deputy Marshal Earp's. Behan captured one of the robbers, brought him back to jail, and then let him escape. When Earp got back to town, he discovered that the sheriff had also framed Doc as the leader of the holdup. Although Wyatt cleared Holliday, he desperately wanted to get the credit for capturing the thieves. So he went to a small-time bandit, Ike Clanton, who was a friend of the fugitives and offered him the reward money to betray their hideout. But before Earp could act, the holdup men were killed. Shortly thereafter the Clanton deal became common gossip and Ike accused the deputy marshal of spreading lies about him. The Clanton brothers—Ike and Billy—got their friends to side with them against the Earps and with Behan. Thus the scene was set for the most famous man-to-man gunfight in the annals of the frontier: the battle at the OK Corral. (Interestingly enough, the thirty second shoot-out occurred in an empty lot behind the corral, not in it.) Early on the morning of October 26, 1881, word reached Earp that the Clantons and three friends were waiting for him. Virgil, Wyatt, Morgan and Doc accepted the challenge with Holliday carrying a sawed-off shotgun. Ike Clanton, the originator of the battle, fled before anything got started, but his nineteen-year-old brother was killed along with two other friends.

The following day, Behan issued warrants for the Earps and Holliday, but the men were cleared of any wrongdoings. However, their trouble was still not over. On the night of December 28, Virgil was ambushed and maimed for life, and three months later Morgan was murdered. Wyatt, along with Doc, went after the killers, getting three of them in less than a week, and then left Tombstone for good. It marked the end of the famous, wild frontier towns with only a few of the bad men still terrorizing the territory.

Around these details, director Kahn fashioned in *Law and Order* a realistic melodrama about a lawman named Frame Johnson, who came to cleanup Tombstone, but leaves in the end, weary of killing, realizing that his gunfighting days have yet to go on. One of the better scenes involved the peace officer reluctantly hanging a young cowpuncher (Andy Devine) for an accidental murder, but the greatest excitement occurred in the last reel when the relatively actionless movie turned into a shooting spree with the gunfight in the town's corral, aided considerably by some very fine camerawork.

An interesting sidelight had to do with Walter Brennan, a minor actor in the film, who fourteen years later, and after three academy awards for supporting roles, would give one of his greatest performances as "Old Man" Clanton in *My Darling Clementine*.

Law and Order marked the end of the important Westerns for the time being, and the major studios stopped making spectacular frontier stories, particularly realistic ones. And there was a very good reason why! The country had been hit by a great depression near the end of 1929, and many people, out-of-work and seeking escape from their dismal daily lives, wanted romance, not harsh stories.

At first, the stock market crash hadn't affected the movie industry, but by 1932 almost all the studios were undergoing tremendous reorganizations. Lasky had lost everything in the crash and was out of Paramount. Fox, too, had been wiped out, and by the next year his slumping firm would merge with the recently-formed but highly successful Twentieth Century Company, run by David Selznick. Then there was Laemmle, whose holdings began to fall apart, and after four years he was forced out of the industry for good. In fact, most of the important pioneers of film—stars, directors, and studio heads—were fast disappearing from the ranks of Hollywood's mighty.

Only the producers of Poverty Row grew stronger. Now, more than ever, distributors and exhibitors welcomed inexpensive, exciting "B" movies which could lure people back to theaters as second features in a two-for-the-price-of-one-ticket bargain.

Up to 1940, the most popular and profitable product of these small studios was the serial, a chapter-by-chapter account of individuals facing incredible dangers and adventures. During its long history dating back to 1912, the western serial had proved to be the most enduring form of "cliff-hanger." And in the days of sound, these Saturday afternoon short thrillers provided the stairway for many popular stars of Hollywood, as one authority put it, those going up and those on the way down. The casts read like a who's who of cowboy history: Buck Jones, Harry Carey, Tom Tyler, Johnny Mack Brown, Bill Elliot, Tom Mix, Ken Maynard, Buster Crabbe, Clayton Moore, Rod Cameron and an ex-Texan from Chicago.

The story is told how Nat Levine, the guiding genius behind Mascot Studios, received a series of letters in 1933 from a Chicago radio station singing cowboy. The singer wanted to be in movies and finally convinced Levine, who was having his problems with Ken Maynard back in Hollywood, to give him a chance. So the ex-Texan was brought to California for $100 per week with his sidekick, Smiley Burnette, who received $75 per week. But when they got to Mascot, it took almost a year before they made their first serial; Gene Autry had to learn how to ride and act.

While Autry was being tutored, Levine tried to devise a suitable debut for him. According to one account, the producer, under the influence of a dentist's anesthetic, "dreamed an astounding story about a lost race of supermen, dwelling in underground caverns." From that idea came one of the weirdest western serials in the history of movies: *The Phantom Empire*, twelve chapters of science-fiction, frontier action, and some say the start of the singing cowboys. Actually, Ken Maynard had been singing songs in his pictures for the last five years, trying to create a new western image for himself.

Autry's good fortune brought Roy Rogers to Hollywood a few years later. It also influenced a new trend in moving

99

pictures. Cowboys had always appeared with a favorite horse; now they began developing lasting friendships: Gene rode with Smiley, Roy with "Gabby" Hayes.

The clever film makers reasoned that if two sidekicks were popular, three would be even more popular. Beginning in 1935, and lasting until the end of the Forties, studios teamed-up the young and the old in a series of "B" features that enjoyed considerable popularity. These included such favorites as "The Hopalong Cassidy" group, William Boyd, James Ellison and Al St. John; "The Three Mesquiteers" clan which over the years included such favorites as Bob Livingston, Ray Corrigan, John Wayne, Ralph Byrd and Bob Steel, and "The Rough Riders," starring Buck Jones, Tim McCoy and Raymond Hatton.

Another important development occurred in 1935. Several of the producers of Poverty Row, including Levine, had merged their holdings to form Republic Pictures. By 1939, we were in what many film historians call "the golden age" of the chapter plays. Every Saturday you might see such heroes as Fred Harmon's delightful comic strip creation, Red Ryder, with his Indian companion, Little Beaver; Johnston McCulley's famous Zorro; or Zane Grey's popular King of the Royal Mounted Police.

But the most famous of them all came from the minds of George Trendle and Fran Striker, who had created the story of a masked man and his faithful Indian friend for their Detroit radio audience. Across the world, people thrilled to the hoofbeats of a famous white horse and the cry of "Hi yo, Silver, away!" It soon got to be a standing joke that the definition of an intellectual was someone who could listen to the William Tell overture—the theme music for the series—and not think of *The Lone Ranger*.

The Westerns had once more gained a stronghold in the movie world.

100

Into the lives of the homesteaders (Jean Arthur and Van Heflin) rides a mysterious gunfighter (Alan Ladd) who helps them solve their problems with the cattlemen in George Stevens's *Shane* (1953).

(BETTMANN/SPRINGER FILM ARCHIVE)

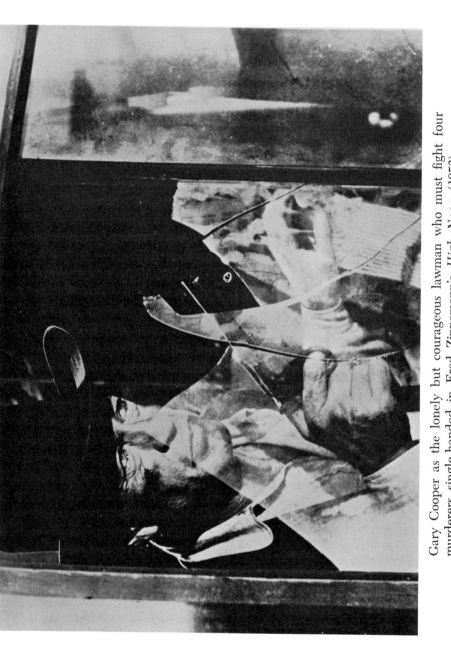

Gary Cooper as the lonely but courageous lawman who must fight four murderers single-handed in Fred Zinnemann's *High Noon* (1952).

J. Carrol Naish plays the great Indian chief who in praying for the dead, vows his hatred for Custer in Sidney Salkow's *Sitting Bull* (1954).

(UNITED ARTISTS)

Robert Wagner, the half-breed son of a domineering man who sets brother against brother, stands before his father's portrait in Edward Dmytryk's *Broken Lance* (1954). (TWENTIETH CENTURY-FOX)

Burt Lancaster as the abused Masai, forced into violence in Robert Aldrich's *Apache* (1954). (UNITED ARTISTS)

Shooting Anthony Mann's *The Man From Laramie* (1955). James Stewart, to the right of the boom, portrays a tough cowboy who withstands the forces of a vicious town.

Julie London and Gary Cooper in a scene from Anthony Mann's *Man of the West* (1960), an interesting yarn about an ex-gunfighter (Cooper) who has to kill his uncle (Lee J. Cobb). Director Mann is wearing the white sport shirt. (UNITED ARTISTS)

Seven strange men band together to help some poor farmers against a vicious group of killers in John Sturges's *The Magnificent Seven*. From left to right: Steve McQueen, James Coburn, Horst Buchholz, Yul Brynner, Brad Dexter, Robert Vaughn and Charles Bronson. (UNITED ARTISTS)

John T. Chance (John Wayne) runs into more woman than he can handle in Feathers (Angie Dickinson), the outspoken and beautiful girl of the West in Howard Hawks's *Rio Bravo* (1959).

(*left*) Paul Newman portrays the legendary Billy the Kid as a psychologically disturbed killer in Arthur Penn's *The Left-Handed Gun* (1958).

THE TALL MEN

Although box-office receipts began declining once again at the end of the Thirties, few people in Hollywood realized the great hardships the Industry had yet to face. And why should they? Movies had survived the business wars, recovered from the effects of the sound revolution and had withstood the worst days of the great Depression. Why should anyone suspect that within a few years the studios, the stars, the very structure of the film world—production, distribution and exhibition—would be in for the greatest revolution of them all? And for certain no one doubted the selling power of western movies. Hollywood was producing more than five hundred feature films a year, of which one hundred were frontier stories. The only surprise with the "A" western movie in the last couple of years had been Cecil B. De Mille's 1937 spectacular *The Plainsman*, starring Gary Cooper as Hickok and Jean Arthur as Calamity Jane. The controversial director had broken with the tradition of the romantic tales of the West, and had his hero die at the end. Then came 1939, probably the greatest year yet in the production of high-grade Westerns.

On Friday, January 13, Twentieth Century-Fox premiered director Henry King's *Jesse James* at the Roxy theater. Here for the first time was an important picture about the most famous outlaws of the old West. Using Nunnally Johnson's clever script, King portrayed Jesse and Frank James, along with the Younger brothers—Jim, Cole and Bob—as Robin Hoods who protected the poor farmers from being exploited by the inhuman bankers and railroad men from the East.

In actuality, the reason that the James gang only stole from the rich was because the farmers had no money. King's real life hero had started his career under the watchful eyes of perhaps America's most vicious criminal, Charles Quantrill. During the Civil War, Frank and Jesse rode with Quantrill's guerrillas, raiding, looting and massacring. Jesse acquired not only a remarkable reputation but also a carefully collected band of outlaws, including the Youngers, who specialized in robberies and murder. At first, the citizens of Missouri cheered the exploits of the daring bandits who almost daily terrorized the "Yankee banks and railroads." It soon became evident that here was no vengeful Southerner, but a vicious and selfish murderer who hurt the state and the economy. As a result, Jesse lost his popularity with the people.

By 1882, the railroads had put up a ten thousand dollar reward for the capture of the outlaw. Soon after, a secret meeting was held between the state's governor and Charles Ford, one of Jesse's friends. On the morning of April 3, Charles and his brother Bob came to the home of Mr. Howard, an alias for the bandit leader, and while Jesse was fixing a picture hanging on the wall, Robert Ford shot him in the back. So much for the glamorous history of the American Robin Hood.

The movie version, except for its heroic treatment of the James gang, did a fine job with its Technicolor representations of the towns and ranches of a romantic West, but the best part of the picture came from the extraordinary cast delivering some pointed dialogue: Tyrone Power as the brave outlaw; Henry Fonda, the sensitive brother; Henry Hull, the outspoken editor who defended the James brothers; and Brian Donlevy, the convincing villain. Another version of the movie made in 1957, was a disaster and is best avoided.

¶ But if the moviegoers liked *Jesse James*, they loved John Ford's new Western, *Stagecoach*, which two months later opened at the fabulous Radio City Music Hall. This all-time cowboy classic brought Ford's directing talents to a peak, and at the same time, made use of what may be the most well-balanced cast of performers ever to ride west together. Dudley Nichols' marvelous script centered around eight passengers on the Overland Stage from Tonto, Arizona, to Lordsburg, New Mexico, during an impending Indian attack. And what a group it was: Dr. Josiah Boone (Thomas Mitchell), the rumpot physician; Major Hatfield (John Carradine), professional cardshark and gentleman of the Old South; Dallas (Claire Trevor), a professional woman who had just lost her redlight apartment in Tonto; Mrs. Lucy Malloy (Louise Platt), refined, pregnant and racing to her husband's side; Henry Gatewood (Berton Churchill), the pompous, long-winded banker who was fleeing with stolen funds; Samuel Peacock (David Meed), unfortunate whiskey salesman who found himself traveling with one of the West's worst drunks; and Sheriff Curley Wilcox (George Bancroft) with his prisoner the Ringo Kid (John Wayne). To top everything off, Andy Devine played Buck, the hungry and bumbling stage driver.

⊦ With this incredible assortment of misfits and his first use of the magnificent Monument Valley as a setting, John Ford provided us with a reminder that sometimes society's best citizens are its outcasts. Of course, there was a shoot out at the end, but some clever fans chuckled when the friendly New

Mexico sheriff let the Kid and Dallas ride off to a border retreat. It reminded them of another Kid they had known. After
this one, however, John Wayne became one of the film world's
greatest cowboy stars, playing one tough westerner after
another.

In the middle of 1939, cowboy pictures were being made
everywhere and with some of the most unusual people. James
Cagney and Humphrey Bogart, for example, had the best
time. They were co-starring in Warner Brothers' *The Oklahoma Kid,* and the two men did not stop laughing during the
entire filming. These former kids from the streets of New York
got hysterical everytime they put on their cowboy outfits and
guns.

The best test of how seriously people take a subject is
whether a good satire can be made of the situation. And near
the end of 1939, Universal Pictures released one of the best
western satires ever, *Destry Rides Again.* The source of the
comedy was writer Max Brand, originator of many of the old
Tom Mix stories and creator of the Dr. Kildare character. This
time, however, he fashioned the tale of how one man tamed
the terrible town of Bottleneck. It seems that the saloon gang
needed a stupid sheriff to cover up their illegal activities, so
they elected the drunken "Wash" Dimsdale to office. But the
old man fooled them and warned everyone that he had sent
for the son of his former fighting companion: Thomas Destry,
Jr. But the men at the Bloody Gulch Saloon got a good laugh
when Destry showed up as a book-toting lawman. Tom tries
to bring law and order through reason but Frenchy, the barroom beauty, argues against it. Then Wash is killed and Tom
returns to his room, puts on his father's guns, and ends the
discussion.

The marvelous thing about the movie was the delightful
typecasting of the studio. Brian Donlevy played his usual
villainous role, while Marlene Dietrich, fought, sang and
loved her way into the audience's hearts. Best of all, James

Stewart, playing the clumsy and sincere lawman, offered an excellent contrast to the silent, strong, and graceful cowboy heroes portrayed by Cooper, Power, Fonda and Wayne.

But no one was laughing in the film world by the end of the year. Profits were less than two-thirds of what they had been in 1938, and with the war in Europe, the industry's important foreign market had been cut off, further reducing profits. To make matters worse, the federal government had ordered that the practice of block booking be stopped—only five films could now be bought at one time and these had to be previewed by the exhibitors first. In addition, Washington gave notice that the studios would have to rid themselves of their large theater chains, since the current arrangements constituted a monopoly. And in Hollywood, many of the skilled and talented performers began organizing themselves into powerful labor unions. In short, the movie industry had rising unemployment, large cuts in salaries, falling profits, and reduced production schedules. "B" Westerns, as a result, grew in popularity as once more the big frontier stories got put to one side.

ǀAlthough Walter Brennan won his third Academy Award in 1940 for his memorable characterization of the ornery Judge Roy Bean in William Wyler's *The Westerner*, the more significant picture of the next two years dealt with the romanticized story of Custer. It was probably the last time that the vain and ambitious soldier, who used the Indian wars to further his political aspirations for the Presidency, would be given a favorable screen image, but Errol Flynn in *They Died with Their Boots on* did the job beautifully. Years later, Ford would retell the same basic story in *Fort Apache* (1948). In this film version, the vain and ambitious colonel (Henry Fonda) rejects the advice of his executive officer (John Wayne) and leads his troops into a fatal encounter with the rebellious Indians. After *Fort Apache*, Ford decided to explore further the life of the cavalry in the Far West and made

112

She Wore A Yellow Ribbon (1949) and *Rio Grande* (1950). The former depicted the last days of command for an elderly colonel (John Wayne) while the latter recounted the difficulties of a soldier's career and the effect that the army had on a man's family. All three films shared the traditional virtues of a Ford Western: visual splendor, charming sentiment, and heroic characters. Together, they formed the greatest trilogy in motion picture history about the dog-faced soldiers who policed the frontier.

By 1943, America was in the midst of her greatest war and the country preferred its escapist Westerns in "B" pictures and serials. Consequently, it was unusual for Twentieth Century-Fox to be making a tense and gripping Western about justice with violence. In fact, the director, William Wellman, only agreed to do the film if he got his choice on his next picture. The trade was agreed to, and *The Ox-bow Incident* went into production. Except for the obvious studio "outdoor" shots, Walter Van Tilburg's perceptive book became a remarkable motion picture account of three cowboys lynched by a strange and unprincipled mob. Even more surprising for Western fans was the fact that there were no heroes and no justice at the end.

By the time many of America's troops had returned from World War II, a new type of atmosphere had taken hold in Hollywood. Strikes had closed down many of the studios in 1945, resulting in a reduction in motion picture production and a 25 percent hike in salaries for studio employees. For the first time in American film history, the foreign market was seriously challenging the United States as the movie center of the world, and in 1947, the House Un-American Activities Committee began their infamous investigation of alleged communists in the movie world. No one remained untouched by the events, and a disturbing crisis emerged in motion picture making. Pictures of the day reflected the mood with an emphasis on violence, mental illness and sex.

113

The groundwork for the first lustful Western had been laid in 1940 by multi-millionaire Howard Hughes, who later gained control of RKO. He had commissioned Howard Hawks, one of the most underrated directors in motion picture history, to do a new version of the Billy Bonney story. This time the focus of attention was on a nineteen year old beauty with unusual physical attributes: Jane Russell. Although *The Outlaw* was first shown in 1943, the Hays office had it removed from public view in America for three years. By today's standards the sexual allusions are quite tame, but back in the Forties when Miss Russell agreed to keep the shivering Billy warm with body heat, censors went berserk.

One of the studios that refused to distribute *The Outlaw*, even though it was obviously going to be a big moneymaker, was run by David Selznick. He had his mind set on producing a great Western of his own, one that turned out to be the strangest cowboy production of all time. The complete story of the filming is told in Bob Thomas's informative biography *Selznick*. In brief, the producer was worried that he would only be remembered for his triumphant *Gone with the Wind*. Lest that should happen, Selznick decided to make an "artistic Western" and hired King Vidor to direct *Duel in the Sun*. (Eventually movie wags referred to it as "Lust in the Dust" or "The Outlaw in Bad Taste.") But no matter what Vidor tried, Selznick had a better idea for the picture that was starring the woman he loved: Jennifer Jones. Consequently it cost more money and took longer to make this Selznick picture than any other. Eventually the audience sat through more than two hours of movie time to watch a torrid romance of two angry Texas brothers (Gregory Peck and Joseph Cotten) trying to win the love of a half-breed Indian girl (Jennifer Jones), with death being the end result. Near the conclusion of the filming, Vidor became so upset by the constant interruptions of Selznick that he got up in the middle of a scene, walked quietly over to the excited producer and said, "You can take this picture and shove it." Vidor never returned. William Dieterle finished the last scenes of the film, while Dimitri Tiomkin came in to write the musical score.

A sneak preview revealed to Selznick that the critics would not like the picture, so the inventive man began the most expensive advertising campaign ever done for a western movie. Furthermore, to outfox the film reviewers whose comments would mean disaster for *Duel in the Sun,* the producer created a new type of distribution: saturation booking. This meant that a number of prints of the picture would be made and released to dozens of theaters on the same day. Consequently, the publicity would be spread throughout the country and the public could see the film before the reviews had a chance to circulate. The result was that the Selznick Western became the fifth biggest moneymaker in cowboy movie history.

/ Despite profits and innovations with sex in Westerns, the great outdoor movie of the Forties was a return to the days of John Chisum and the first big cattle drive across the Rio Grande. Once more Hawks got a chance to show his brilliance in a Frontier setting. In addition to making Montgomery Clift a star in his first screen appearance, *Red River* presented a psychological story about two men, Tom Dunson (John Wayne) and Matthew Garth (Clift), whose hates and loves helped create a cattle empire. No story of the tortuous trail drives ever surpassed Hawks's film, filled with the courage and endurance of individuals who learned to conquer men, cattle and themselves. Some critics have referred to *Red River* as the first "adult Western" because it emphasizes the complexity of men's lives rather than their love for violence.

If 1948 produced the best Western of the decade, it sounded the death bell for the "B" features and the serials. Television had begun to pull audiences away from the theaters, and former cowboy Bill Boyd began making western history on TV by recreating his famous "Hopalong Cassidy" role. If "Hoppy" was a good drawing card, Gene Autry was a great businessman. Beginning with his own TV show, the energetic singing cowboy soon put most of his money and time into a new production unit called the Flying A. Kids everywhere watched hypnotized as the movie heroes of yesterday's shows became the tube's stars of today: The Lone Ranger, The Cisco Kid, and The Roy Rogers Show.

Now what could the movie Western do to survive?

Marlon Brando (Rio) in his film *One-Eyed Jacks* (1963). The ace-of-hearts in the Mona Lisa's hand symbolized the two personalities of the hero: one visible, one hidden.   (PARAMOUNT)

Gil Westrum (Randolph Scott) and Steve Judd (Joel McCrea) are two ex-lawmen who sit around the campfire discussing the value of honesty in a heartless world in Sam Peckinpah's *Ride the High Country* (1961).

(BETTMANN/SPRINGER FILM ARCHIVE)

"Whiskey," Kirk Douglas's horse, reels at the sudden and violent sound of the rotor blades of a U. S. Air Force helicopter in David Miller's *Lonely Are the Brave* (1962). (BETTMANN/SPRINGER FILM ARCHIVE)

James Stewart, a mountain man of the Far West, stops at the corrupt cave-store run by Walter Brennan and his daughter, Brigid Brazlen, in *How the West Was Won* (1964). (BETTMANN/SPRINGER FILM ARCHIVE)

Kid Shelleen (Lee Marvin) and Cat Ballou (Jane Fonda) listen to what has happened to the Hole-in-the-Wall Gang in *Cat Ballou*.
(COPYRIGHT © 1965 COLUMBIA PICTURES CORPORATION)

James Stewart plays the tenderfoot lawyer who gains fame by "killing" Liberty Valance (Lee Marvin). John Wayne does the actual shooting in Ford's *The Man Who Shot Liberty Valance* (1962).

John Wayne satirizes his tough rugged frontiersman image as Rooster, the one-eyed lawman, in Henry Hathaway's *True Grit* (1969).

Four men ride out to bring back a missing woman in Richard Brooks's *The Professionals* (1966). Three of these expert gunmen are from left to right: Woody Strode, Lee Marvin and Burt Lancaster.

Paul Newman as the white man brought up by Indians in Martin Ritt's first Western, *Hombre* (1967). (TWENTIETH CENTURY-FOX)

The story of what happens to the gunfighters who have lived beyond the times that made them is violently presented in Sam Peckinpah's *The Wild Bunch* (1969). The doomed men, from left to right: Ben Johnson, Warren Oates, William Holden and Ernest Borgnine.

(WARNER BROTHERS/SEVEN ARTS)

Eva Marie Saint portrays the white mother of an Indian child, and Gregory Peck acts as their sympathetic friend in Robert Mulligan's *The Stalking Moon* (1969). (WARNER-PATHÉ)

GROWING OLD

As the era of the massive studio system rapidly came to an end, a new brand of Western emerged. The film makers rightly reasoned that no one would pay for old formulas when they could freely flick on the television to see Ken Maynard, Buck Jones and Bill Boyd. However, if the movie houses presented an unusual frontier story, one found nowhere else, that might induce the patrons back into the dwindled audience. Although some executives continued to ignore this theory, the smarter ones began switching to the "adult" western concept, sometimes referred to as the "psychological" or "mature" cowboy movie. The concept had been tried before, but never like this.

 On June 7, 1950, Universal-International released *Winchester '73*, the first of a highly successful string of feature films by the talented combination of director Anthony Mann and actor James Stewart. Others would include such pictures as *Bend of the River* (1952) and *The Man From Laramie* (1955). The original film, however, helped set the trend for the "adult" cowboy dramas in the Fifties. On the surface, the

124

plot typified Mann's emphasis on conflict and a strong story. This one dealt with an angry, rugged cowboy (Stewart) pursuing his enemies and determined to recover a stolen rifle. *Winchester '73* also emphasized the director's usual concern for exciting pictorial qualities which could help simplify his scripts and reduce the amount of dialogue spoken in his movies. But screenwriter Bordon Chase had mixed into the story's violent episodes some biting pieces of humor which indicated cynicism more than comedy. Furthermore, the hard-bitten hero shared a very strange and complex relationship with his enemies, suggesting that his actions were more psychological than simple acts of justice. In fact, Stewart, in several scenes, acted no differently in deed or action from those he opposed. What's more, this "adult" cowboy wanted no part of idealistic values. His past experiences had taught him that anything was permissible so long as it kept you alive and brought results.

That same month, Twentieth Century-Fox premiered Henry King's anti-tradition Western, *The Gunfighter*, a stunning examination of a once popular frontier killer. The story centered on Jimmy Ringo, a fast gun who, old and tired, wanted nothing better than to put away his pistols and be reunited with his family. But it wasn't possible. In a dozen dirty barrooms in countless dusty towns, young, aspiring "squirts" wanted to make a reputation for themselves by killing the famous gunfighter. King brought the various characters together in a single setting, and using the classical elements of time, place, and action, presented the sad predicament of the Ringos. Gregory Peck gave a memorable performance as the wistful fast gun, supported admirably by Jean Parker, the understanding saloon girl; Millard Mitchell, the sympathetic lawman; Karl Malden, the shrewd barkeeper; and Helen Westcott, the grief-stricken wife.

Two years later, the theme of the tired plainsman, who had long since lost the innocence of youthful idealism, reached screen greatness in Fred Zinnemann's *High Noon*. What made

125

this treatment so unusual was the director's presentation of western types rather than actual individuals. Aided by Carl Foreman's beautiful screenplay, Zinnemann filmed the story of a weary, stubborn sheriff in a lonesome frontier town on the day of his marriage and retirement. Soon after the wedding, Will Kane learns that a killer he once sent to jail has been pardoned and is coming back on the noon train for revenge. Everyone argues that the Sheriff should leave town, but Kane decides otherwise. He seeks support from the various elements in the community in his impending face-to-face showdown with the Frank Miller gang. Every group—social, political, economic and religious—refuses to help, preferring instead to sacrifice the life of one man rather than face possible personal danger. (Few people in 1952 realized how clearly Foreman's script reflected his personal crisis with the House Un-American Activities Committee and the unwillingness of citizens to become involved or take a stand on the issues.)

At a sneak preview of *High Noon*, Stanley Kramer, the producer, realized that the film lacked a powerful tension, one necessary to hold the various episodes together. He took the print to the editing room and over a series of weeks worked into the movie a number of shots of a large town clock indicating the passing of time. He also added the voice of the former cowboy star, Tex Ritter, singing the ballad of "High Noon." When the film was finally distributed to the public, it received tremendous acclaim. Besides serving as a valuable statement on modern times, the story of Will Kane restored the slumping popularity of Gary Cooper and earned the star his second Academy Award.

But the theme of the tired cowboy was not played out yet. Within a year, director George Stevens and screenwriter A. B. Guthrie, Jr. combined their talents to make *Shane*. Taken from Jack Schaffer's novel about a young boy's experience with a mysterious gunfighter, the film story seemed deceptively simple. The setting is Wyoming in 1890 where a feud exists be-

126

tween the cattlemen and the homesteader. On one side is Ryker (Emile Meyer), the old frontiersman, who for decades has withstood man and nature to establish his cattle empire. On the other side are the Starretts, recently arrived from the East and stubbornly determined to take root on free land. But the "sod busters" need to fence in the range to grow their crops, and Ryker refuses to allow this to happen. Into this conflict between the old and the new rides a mysterious stranger, Shane (Alan Ladd), who is looking for an escape from a violent past. Shane sides with the poor farmers, eventually endearing himself to Joe Starrett (Van Heflin), Mrs. Starrett (Jean Parker), and their nine year old son (Brandon de Wilde). Tension builds when Joe and Shane best Ryker's men in a barroom fight, and the cattle baron sends for a professional killer, Wilson (Jack Palance), to help end the feud. Soon after Wilson's arrival, he shoots down one of the homesteaders and the farmers begin to panic. Although Joe feels he is the one to face the hired gunman, Shane realizes that he alone has the skill to defend his friends. Unfortunately for the tired gunfighter, he feels compelled to put on his pistols and ride into town, leaving behind any hope of the peace he so desperately wanted. In the dimly-lit barroom the men of a bygone era gather. Ryker taunts Shane by telling him that he is "a dead man." And Shane replies, "That's the difference between us; I know it." Afterwards, Shane rides off into the night, wounded and knowing that trouble and death constitute his future.

The picture had everything to delight the audience: a creative sound track, realistic settings, lovely visual effects and superb editing which kept the viewers on the edge of their seats waiting for the classic showdown. Furthermore, Alan Ladd as the mythic gunfighter and Jack Palance as his vicious counterpart established two of the most remarkable fast guns in western screen history.

Before we go too far, we ought to note that the film makers had also changed their attitude toward the American Indian.

f Except for some of the early silent films of Griffith, Ince and Hart, Red Men had been nothing more than animals to be hunted down or shot off horses and sinister-looking cliffs at the appropriate moment. On July 20, 1950, Twentieth Century-Fox destroyed that image with Delmar Daves' *Broken Arrow*. Although it was not a particularly well-done film—his two best Westerns being *3:10 To Yuma* (1957) and *Cowboy* (1958)—the story opened up a whole new tradition for frontier films. Based upon Elliot Arnold's sprawling historical novel *Blood Brother*, the screenplay dealt with James Stewart as Tom Jefferds, Civil War veteran, who comes to live among the Chiricahua Apaches and marries one of their women. Afterwards he tried to bring peace between the settlers and his Indian brothers, but too often the white man's bigotry and Geronimo's hatred seem destined to destroy the peace treaty. Only the wisdom and strength of Cochise (Jeff Chandler) offer hope to both sides. This was quite an unusual depiction of the Indian.

M-G-M then released its attempt at reversing the once popular tradition of downgrading Indians, Anthony Mann's *Devil's Doorway*. This underrated film, and too often neglected performance by Robert Taylor, clearly attacked the prejudices and greed of certain American pioneers. Woven into the fictional biography of Lance Poole, a Shoshone Indian who had been awarded the Congressional Medal of Honor for his bravery at the battle of Gettysburg, are the hardships of a Red Man who wants to find peace and raise cattle near Medicine Bow, Wyoming. (It's important to remember that the hometown of the Virginian was there, indicating a direct attack on the formulas of the pure, saintly cowboys of old.) Sheepmen, lawyers and ignorant people all combine to kill the proud Indian who refuses to be chased from the land that was rightfully his.

After these two films, movies presenting more sympathetic characterizations of the American Indian became quite fashionable and big stars like Burt Lancaster, Rock Hudson and

Paul Newman readily appeared in sympathetic roles of mistreated Red Men. Among the most popular moving pictures in this area have been *Sitting Bull, Apache,* and *Broken Lance* (all in 1954), *The Unforgiven* (1960), *Cheyenne Autumn* (1964), *Tell Them Willie Boy Is Here* (1969) and *A Man Called Horse* (1970). It is important that popularity should not be confused with quality, nor good intentions with accomplishments. The stories are still romanticized accounts by white men about what they feel and know about Indians. To date there has not been a single film which has presented a direct and honest treatment of the plight of the American Red Man from the Indian's point of view. Until that time, the screen will remain suspect in its desire to honestly show the full story of the West.

Near the middle of the Fifties, Walt Disney's TV production of *Davy Crockett* convinced the heads of the major television networks that Westerns could not only succeed in prime time slots, but also would be worth having in large numbers. And so the TV world began its long and uneven career in the production of such sagebrush shows as *Wyatt Earp, Cheyenne, Broken Arrow, Gunsmoke* and *Maverick.* Within a short time there appeared *Rawhide, Wagon Train, Have Gun Will Travel, Wanted Dead or Alive, The Westerner* and *Bonanza.*

As the big western movies continued to do well as the box-office and the television studios expanded their production of cowboy stories, the men of Poverty Row gradually disappeared from the film world. Unions, producing costs, and a declining popularity at the box-office, all contributed to the "B" pictures' collapse. There was, however, one major exception.

Director Budd Boetticher joined actor Randolph Scott and began making a group of unconventional low-budget Westerns, probably some of the best ever made. Capitalizing on the familiar conventions of the "B" film—action and violence—the new productions introduced a more cynical approach to frontier life. Beginning with *Seven Men From Now* in 1956 and including such films as *The Tall T* (1957), *Decision at Sundown* (1957), *Buchanan Rides Again* (1958), *Ride Lonesome* (1959) and *Commance Station* (1960), audiences watched Scott portray a variety of men who dared to gamble against what appeared to be insurmountable odds, yet believed they had no other choice. What makes it most interesting was that these defiant heroes stood alone, without idealistic values, tradition or friends.

By 1958, the success of the "A" Westerns began to reverse itself. The concept of the belligerent, neurotic cowboy proved particularly unpopular in Arthur Penn's underrated film *The Left-Handed Gun*. Once more we saw the aftermath of the Lincoln County wars, only this time Billy Bonney was played by a graduate of New York's Actors' Studio. This training school emphasized "method" acting, a technique which stressed realistic acting. Consequently, Paul Newman portrayed Billy the Kid as a lonely, frustrated and mentally-disturbed individual who belonged to no one and nowhere. Critics and fans objected not only to the film's slow-pace, but to the strange, unexplained mannerisms of Newman's characterization.

That same year, director William Wyler finished *The Big Country*, the story of an Easterner's success in the rugged frontier setting. Gregory Peck played the part of the strong, silent tenderfoot who proved that he had to answer to no man, and that an individual's courage could be proven without the help of guns. Although the film included a host of stars like Gregory Peck, Charlton Heston, Burl Ives and Charles Bickford, it tended to be boring and drawn out.

There seemed to be no more major Westerns coming out of Hollywood as the Sixties approached. Then a classic appeared in 1959. Howard Hawks had said for many years that he felt *High Noon* was a foolish picture about a man who wasted a lot of time trying to get help, when in the end he and his

Quaker wife (Grace Kelly) fought the good fight alone. Someone challenged the director to do better, and in the last year of the decade he presented his thrilling and leisurely-paced *Rio Bravo*. The setting is a Texas border town where Sheriff John T. Chance (John Wayne) is determined to hold a ruthless killer prisoner until the U.S. Marshal comes, which won't be until five more days. That might not be such a bad idea, except the man's wealthy and angry relatives don't think much of Chance's plan. Whereas Cooper in *High Noon* refuses help from a cripple, Wayne in *Rio Bravo* accepts it from the maimed deputy portrayed by Walter Brennan. On the other hand, when Cooper asks for help from the able-bodied citizens he gets none, while Wayne never asks and gets help from a drunk (Dean Martin in one of his finest roles) and a young kid (Ricky Nelson). To contrast the Quaker prissiness of Grace Kelly, Hawks creates probably the most wonderful female character ever to make love with a lawman, the quick-witted "Feathers," played magnificently by Angie Dickinson.

Unfortunately, *Rio Bravo* proved the exception rather than the rule for the production of Westerns for the next three years. In 1960, John Wayne produced, starred and directed in a twelve-million-dollar tribute to the brave men who had, in 1836, saved Texas from falling into the hands of the Mexicans. *The Alamo* was poorly edited and not even the romantic, hero-worshipping characterizations of Davy Crockett and Jim Bowie could make the film a critical success. Yet like *Duel in the Sun*, this blockbuster brought enough patrons to the box-office to make it one of the biggest money-makers in western film history.

One year later, Marlon Brando directed and starred in a clear-cut imitation of the Billy Bonney story, *One-Eyed Jacks*. The film had been started and stopped a number of times, with the original director, Stanley Kubrick, making several movies during the delays and then finally being fired from the production. Brando played the part of the Rio Kid who had served time in prison because his partner, Dad (Karl Malden, still another graduate of the Actors' Studio) had betrayed him. By the time Rio catches up with his partner, Dad has become a lawman in California. Before Rio gets his revenge, fans are treated to a number of conventional scenes: a bank robbery and a posse's pursuit, a mysterious stranger riding alone into a hostile setting, the possibility of a lynching, and the final gunfight in the center of town. In addition to the psychological suggestion of having the treacherous lawman called "Dad," *One-Eyed Jacks* presents an intriguing and original slant to the Bonney-Garrett relationship, although Brando does concern himself far more with his stylized acting than with the telling of the story.

In 1962, cowboy films suddenly found themselves having their greatest season since 1950. Director John Sturges released his hilarious satire *Sergeants 3*, a devastating attack on the old cavalry movies. Sammy Davis, Jr., in particular, did a good job as a self-sacrificing soldier, much in the manner of the native hero in *Gunga Din*.

In May, Ford released his last great Western, *The Man Who Shot Liberty Valance*. Once more we had the director's romantic story-telling qualities, but this time filled with some of the most brilliant scenes Ford had ever put together. The story, told mostly in flashback, concerned Ransom Stoddard (James Stewart), a naïve Eastern lawyer who comes to the wild town of Shinbone, intending, by the use of reason, to bring civilization to the West. Before very long, Ransom is the sworn enemy of the meanest man in the territory, Liberty Valance (Lee Marvin), in love with the beautiful Hallie (Vera Miles), and the friend of the individualistic Tom Doniphon (John Wayne). Eventually, Ransom is forced into a showdown with Valance, and late one night the lawyer becomes famous for his unexpected killing of the villain. Near the end of the movie we find out that Doniphon, not Ranson, had shot Valance.

Tom loved Hallie, and he knew that the only way to protect Stoddard was to kill Valance. Afterwards, Tom had just wandered aimlessly, missing Hallie's love and companionship, dying alone. There is a superb moment when Ransom checks the coffin and notices that Tom's boots are missing, and tells the undertaker to put them back on.

In late June of '62, Metro released through saturation booking one of the classic frontier films, Sam Peckinpah's *Ride the High Country*. For those who had seen so many of the Randolph Scott and Joel McCrea "B" pictures, this modest movie seemed to sum it all up and put the finishing touch to the images of two men who had outlived their value to the scores of dusty, dirty frontier towns that needed civilizing. Filled with good humor, photographed in brilliant color, and well-acted the screenplay framed the story of the temptations and problems of two retired cowboys who made their living by doing odd and degrading jobs.

Incredible as it may seem, one week later another low-budget screen masterpiece appeared and with just as little recognition as Peckinpah's film: David Miller's *Lonely Are the Brave*. More than any other picture yet made, this excellent film, helped considerably by Dalton Trumbo's script, portrayed the clash of the independent cowboy with the modern world. Walter Matthau gave a brilliant performance as the cynical sheriff who regrets hunting down the uncompromising westerner. And Kirk Douglas plays perfectly the role of the fugitive who has to fight against the technological posse of a helicopter, jeeps and electronics. (Two other films that take up the condition of the cowboy today—*Hud* and *The Misfits*—are really not Westerns in the strictest sense because they present individuals located on the frontier, not living off the land, whose problems are unrelated to the action stories we've been covering.)

Everything done in 1962 was eclipsed the next year, that is, as far as cost is concerned. M-G-M, in association with

Cinerama, overwhelmed the public with a Western which required three directors (John Ford, George Marshall, Henry Hathaway), more than twenty stars, over two thousand animals, and close to thirteen thousand people in the supporting cast. They called it *How the West Was Won*. The motto seemed to be, "What ever you've seen before, we have it here, only bigger, for more money, and with more noise." Nevertheless, the audiences made this movie the number one box-office Western of all time.

After that, laughter and violence became the main attraction for Westerns. In 1965, *Cat Ballou*, in spite of Norman Silverstein's heavy-handed direction, proved it had no equal for satirizing the traditional frontier formula. Following the conventional revenge theme, the screenplay by Walter Newman and Frank Pierson presented Miss Catherine Ballou (Jane Fonda), the innocent school teacher who returns from an Eastern college to find her father defending his land against the vicious railroad agents and their hired gun, Strawn (Lee Marvin). So Catherine, remembering what she has read in the dime novels about the "real" West, hires the famous Kid Shelleen (also played by Marvin). From the time we first meet the drunken, weatherbeaten kid, it's one marvelous gag after another. Shelleen, for example, explains to Cat that the West is changing, that they're putting in a roller skating rink at the OK Corral. Later on, when Cat and her gang ride away from a holdup, they seek refuge with the famous Hole-in-the-Wall gang. But when the meeting takes place, the former wild bunch are old, fat, and frightened of trouble. All the kid can do is drink, and ask "What happened to you?"

Nevertheless, when Strawn threatens Cat, Shelleen decides to live up to his legend and goes into training. Slowly his skill returns and he once more dresses and acts the part of the gallant knight fighting for his lady's honor. After killing his enemy (also his brother), Shelleen returns, asks Cat for her hand in marriage, gets rejected, and goes back to drinking. The film concludes with the kid on his weary, stumbling white horse riding out into the distant horizons. Lee Marvin received a much deserved Academy Award for his dual role in the movie.

/ In 1969, Paramount released director Henry Hathaway's satirical *True Grit,* based upon Charles Portis' best-selling novel. The plot centered around Mattie Ross and her desire to get her father's murderer. The young girl hires the tough, one-eyed marshal, Rooster (John Wayne), to find the killer and bring him in. Although there are some lovely visual shots, the movie suffers from weak acting and bad cutting. However, Wayne ridicules almost every aspect of the legendary image of the tough cowboy he had created over the past forty years. And once more a nostalgic Motion Picture Academy awarded an Oscar to a comic Western hero, this time played by Wayne.

That same year Twentieth Century-Fox unveiled director George Roy Hill's *Butch Cassidy and the Sundance Kid.* Again we saw the story of men who had lived beyond their time, only now the tale was filled with music and comedy. One good sight gag had the two men rob a bank that is no longer in business. Another gag was to have them bungle their dynamiting of a safe so badly that the train and the money got blown up in the explosion.

Yet this comedy knew when to get serious. There is a very poignant moment when Katherine Ross, playing the girl friend, explains, "I'm twenty-six, and I'm single, and I teach school, and that's the bottom of the pit. And the only excitement I've ever known is sitting in the room with me now. So I'll go with you, and I won't whine, and I'll sew your socks and stitch you when you're wounded, anything you ask of me I'll do, except one thing: I won't watch you die." And later on she leaves Butch (Paul Newman) and Sundance (Robert Redford) in Bolivia, just before their fatal ride into a small town where they are ambushed. Unfortunately the movie ends with the men dying bravely, leaving many impressionable people in the audience with the idea that the two bandits were likable fellows. In actuality, Butch and Sundance were two of the most vicious gunmen ever to roam the West. And when Sundance was killed in the ambush, Butch, rather than face capture, put his pistol in his mouth and committed suicide.

⊢ Not everyone was thrilled by these "mature" Westerns, nor for that matter were all the innovations in the cowboy pictures coming from the United States. For years, foreign countries like Spain, Germany, Italy and Japan had been making dozens of sagebrush stories. In fact, Japan's greatest director Akira Kurosawa was responsible for an equally popular trend in the Sixties. In 1956, he had imitated Ford's methods and made an exciting movie called *The Seven Samurai*, the story of an isolated village of farmers who hire seven warriors to protect them against dangerous bandits. John Sturges, four years later, turned it into the first of a series of pictures about a band of outlaws collected to do impossible jobs: *The Magnificent Seven*.

Film producers, using the logic of old, figured that if one collection of killers did good business for a studio, why not collect some tough hombres for other studios. One popular example of this theory was Richard Brooks' *The Professionals* in 1966. The story concerned four professional killers hired by a wealthy businessman to recover his "kidnapped" wife from a revolutionary band in Mexico. But underlying the action was a complete rejection of humane values. When the hired gunmen, for example, kill some men sent out to ambush them, Lee Marvin, the leader of the Professionals, states that the dead men's horses should be killed. Otherwise the animals are going to return to the bandits' camp and alert the outlaws. Robert Ryan argues against the slaughter. But they should have killed the beasts. Marvin's observations were

136

correct. The bandits were alerted. Another example occurs when the men meet an old shepherd, and Marvin suggests that he be killed since there is no way of determining whether the stranger is friend or foe. Again, humane values prevail and the man is spared. If the Professionals had listened to Marvin they would have avoided unnecessary danger. Time and time again, the film argues that the most important thing in life is self-preservation . . . whatever the cost, regardless of traditional morality.

But no single western film in movie history has every been more violent than Sam Peckinpah's *The Wild Bunch* in 1969. The director had failed five years before with his first big-budget Western *Major Dundee,* a badly mutilated account of a union officer forced to join up with a confederate prisoner of war in a pursuit of a raiding Apache band. Now Peckinpah intended to make an "A" picture that would not only depict the horrors of violence, but also reestablish his reputation.

The setting for the movie is Texas in 1914 where the last bad men are being chased out of the country by savage bounty hunters, employed by ruthless railroad and banking interests too important to do their own killing. Right from the first scene, everyone is aware that he is watching the final days of Pike Bishop (William Holden) and his men. As the bandits ride into town to pull a bank robbery, the citizens are waiting for them. In a prolonged and violent massacre, the unmerciful citizens mow down the majority of robbers. Only Pike and a few men escape. Pike manages to escape because Deke Thornton (Robert Ryan) refuses to kill his former associate. The rest of the film details the pursuit of the bandits, and Thornton's realization that it is better to live like Pike than settle for the new West. The end comes when Bishop decides to rob one more bank, even though he knows that it will mean his death. As he says, "I wouldn't have it any other way."

Kurosawa also had an indirect effect on the violence and cynicism of *The Wild Bunch.* In 1961, the brilliant director had made *Yojimbo* (The Bodyguard), a devastating satire about a jobless samurai who hires himself out to protect a silk merchant who is engaged in a terrible and violent rivalry with a saké merchant. Both sides have their share of hoodlums, but the bodyguard eventually wipes everyone out, including his boss and leaves the town "a quieter place." Italy's opportunistic director Sergio Leone liked the plot, the violence and the formula of the deadly stranger and went about translating the comic action into a serious traditional western setting. He hired Clint Eastwood, the handsome, clean-cut star of television's *Rawhide* and made *A Fistful of Dollars* which opened in the United States on February 2, 1967. The production company gave credits to people from Germany, Spain and Italy. The result was that Eastwood started a new trend in violent Westerns as the man with no name who mysteriously rides into a sinister frontier town and takes on its toughest outlaws. And when Peckinpah told interviewers, in 1969, that in *The Wild Bunch* he wanted to take the romance out of killing, he probably was referring to some of the conventions that the Leone Westerns were glamorizing.

By the end of the Sixties, the motion picture industry had come almost full circle in their depiction of the Old West when *Butch Cassidy and the Sundance Kid* appeared. The movie had all the ingredients of the great cowboy formulas: violence, comedy, romance, music and the very outlaws who, at the turn of the century, had suggested the idea for the first Western of them all, *The Great Train Robbery*.

And what can we expect in the Seventies? That will depend in part on the technological advances in the movie world. With changing screen sizes, different projectors, more control over color, and new types of film, Westerns may tell a different story, present a different emphasis. Then too, as the motion picture code becomes more permissive, violence and sex will probably be even more exploited than any of us can imagine. The future will also depend on the way producers, directors,

138

stars, and other important people rearrange the business of making, distributing and exhibiting movies. But despite these changes, I suspect that the old formulas—satire, sentiment, action and heroes—will be with us for many years to come.

Looking back at all the stories and pictures, one gets the feeling that maybe Ford explained it best when it comes to what the public wants. In *The Man who Shot Liberty Valance,* Ransom asks the editor (Edmund O'Brien) what he should do now that he knows the truth of the killing. Dutton Peabody replies, "When the legend becomes fact, print the legend."

BIBLIOGRAPHY

BIBLIOGRAPHY

The author hopes that the following selective book list will aid the interested reader in exploring more fully the history of western movies. Because of this book's brevity, no one writer's opinions were singled out, and for that reason references to specific authors have not been given. Anyone reading the following books, which your author has consulted, will have no difficulty in determining which books were made use of, what was taken from them, and where each went his own way.

Baxter, John. *Hollywood in the Thirties.* New York: A. S. Barnes & Co., 1968.

Bogdanovich, Peter. *John Ford.* Berkeley: University of California Press, 1968.

Carpozi, George, Jr. *The Gary Cooper Story.* New Rochelle, New York: Arlington House, 1970.

Corneau, Ernest N. *The Hall of Fame of Western Film Stars.* North Quincy, Mass.: The Christopher Publishing House, 1969.

De Mille, Cecil B. *Autobiography.* Edited by Donald Hayne. Englewood Cliffs: Prentice-Hall, Inc., 1959.

Dickens, Homer. *The Films of Gary Cooper.* New York: Citadel Press, 1970.

Everson, William K. *A Pictorial History of the Western Film.* New York: Citadel Press, 1969.

Eyles, Allen. *The Western: An Illustrated Guide.* New York: A. S. Barnes & Co., 1967.

Fenin, George N. and William K. Everson. *The Westerns: From Silents to Cinerama.* New York: Bonanza Books, 1962.

Fernett, Gene. *Next Time Drive Off the Cliff!* Cocoa, Fla.: Cinememories Publishing Company, 1968.

_____. *Starring John Wayne.* Cocoa, Fla.: Brevard Printing Company, 1969.

Fredrik, Nathalie. *Hollywood and the Academy Awards.* Beverly Hills: Hollywood Awards Publications, 1970.

French, Philip. *The Movie Moguls: An Informal History of the Hollywood Tycoons.* London: Weidenfeld and Nicolson, 1969.

Gehman, Richard. *The Tall American: The Story of Gary Cooper.* New York: Hawthorn Books, Inc., 1963.

Griffith, Richard, and Arthur Mayer. *The Movies.* Rev. ed. New York: Simon and Schuster, Inc., 1970.

Hampton, Benjamin B., with a new introduction by Richard Griffith. *History of the American Film Industry: From its Beginning to 1931.* New York: Dover Publications, Inc., 1970.

Higham, Charles and Joel Greenberg. *Hollywood in the Forties.* New York: A. S. Barnes & Co., 1968.

Horan, James D. and Paul Sann. *Pictorial History of the Wild West.* New York: Crown Publishers, Inc., 1954.

Jennings, Gary. *The Movie Book.* New York: The Dial Press, 1963.

Kael, Pauline. *I Lost It At the Movies.* New York: Bantam Books, 1965.

Kitses, Jim. *Horizons West.* London: Thames and Hudson in Association with the British Film Institute, 1969.

Lasky, Jesse with Don Weldon. *I Blow My Own Horn.* London: Victor Gollancz Limited, 1957.

Manchel, Frank. *When Pictures Began to Move.* Englewood Cliffs: Prentice-Hall, Inc., 1969.

————. *When Movies Began to Speak.* Englewood Cliffs: Prentice-Hall, Inc., 1969.

Marshall Cavendish Learning System, The. *The Movies.* London: Marshall Cavendish Books, 1970.

Richie, Donald. *George Stevens: An American Romantic.* New York: Museum of Modern Art, 1970.

Robinson, David. *Hollywood in the Twenties.* New York. A. S. Barnes & Co., 1968.

Rosa, Joseph G. *The Gunfighter: Man or Myth?* Norman: University of Oklahoma Press, 1969.

Rosenberg, Bernard and Harry Silverstein. *The Real Tinsel.* New York: the Macmillan Company, 1970.

Scheuer, Steven H., editor. *Movies on TV*. New York: Bantam Books, 1968.

Smith, Henry Nash. *Virgin Land: The American West as Symbol and Myth*. New York: Vintage Books, 1950.

Speed, F. Maurice, editor. *The Western Film Annual*. London: Macdonald & Company, 1955.

_____. *The Western Film and T.V. Annual*. London: Macdonald & Company, 1959–1962.

Steckmesser, Kent Ladd. *The Western Hero in History and Legend*. Norman: University of Oklahoma Press, 1965.

Thomas, Bob. *Selznick*. Garden City, N. Y.: Doubleday & Company, Inc., 1970.

Warman, Eric and Tom Vallance, editors. *Westerns: A Preview Special*. London: Golden Pleasure Books, 1964.

Warshow, Robert. *The Immediate Experience*. Garden City, N. Y.: Anchor Books, 1964.

Wood, Robin. *Howard Hawks*. Garden City, N.Y.: Doubleday & Company, Inc., 1968.

Zukor, Adolph with Dale Kramer. *The Public Is Never Wrong*. New York: G. P. Putnam's Sons, 1953.

INDEX

148

149